Yearbook of the Ayrshire Cattle Breeders for 1908

by Ayrshire Breeders' Association

with an introduction by Jackson Chambers

This work contains material that was originally published in 1908.

This publication is within the Public Domain.

This edition is reprinted for educational purposes
and in accordance with all applicable Federal Laws.

Introduction Copyright 2017 by Jackson Chambers

Self Reliance Books

Get more historic titles on animal and stock breeding, gardening and old fashioned skills by visiting us at:

http://selfreliancebooks.blogspot.com/

Introduction

I am pleased to present another title in the "Cattle" series.

The work is in the Public Domain and is re-printed here in accordance with Federal Laws.

As with all reprinted books of this age that are intended to perfectly reproduce the original edition, considerable pains and effort had to be undertaken to correct fading and sometimes outright damage to existing proofs of this title. At times, this task is quite monumental, requiring an almost total "rebuilding" of some pages from digital proofs of multiple copies. Despite this, imperfections still sometimes exist in the final proof and may detract from the visual appearance of the text.

I hope you enjoy reading this book as much as I enjoyed making it available to readers again.

Jackson Chambers

HOME DAIRY TEST 1906-7.

French Prize Cup Awarded to Geo. H. McFadden, Bryn Mawr, Pa.

Report of the Proceedings

OF THE

Thirty-Third Annual Meeting

OF THE

Ayrshire Breeders' Association

HELD AT

The Fifth Avenue Hotel, New York City

January 15, 1908

The Thirty-third Annual Meeting of the Ayrshire Breeders' Association was held at the Fifth Avenue Hotel, New York City, N. Y., in response to the call of the Secretary, and was called to order at two-thirty p. m. by the President, George William Ballou, who said:

GENTLEMEN AND FELLOW MEMBERS OF THE AYRSHIRE BREEDERS' ASSOCIATION.—This thirty-third annual meeting reminds us that a third of a century has passed since the inception of this Association.

The opening of the great corn belt of the Central Western States and the Mississippi Valley, and the wheat regions of Kansas, Nebraska, Minnesota and the Dakotas, had then just begun; and the era of low price western lands, cheap transportation to the seaboard, of cereals, live stock and all the products of that vast empire of fertile soil, was then well under way.

To all this the farmers of that day in the East, can testify; and they well remember the depression of farm values and the destruction of their revenues in a competition they were then unable to meet. And yet this span of thirty-three years has marked a growth of population and prosperity in this country so great as to invite and command the admiration of the entire civilized world; as shown in the marvellous proportions reached in transportation, manufacturing, stock-raising, and in the output of the mines, forests and farms.

Mr. James J. Hill, one of our members, "a Farmer from Minnesota," as he styled himself at the time of the Northern Pacific corner in Wall Street, demonstrated in his Minnesota State Fair speech in 1906, that, " within twenty years 125,000,000 people, and before the middle of the century, over 200,000,000 people, must find room and employment within the United States."

" That every acre of our public lands possible of cultivation will be absorbed and occupied within fifteen years."

" That of the four sources of wealth, the sea, the forests, the mines (including coal and iron), and the soil,—the sea only furnishes two or three per cent of man's food, and probably will continue; that the great forests east of the Rockies will have entirely disappeared, and the available deposits of both coal and iron will have been mostly exhausted before the middle of this century;—leaving only the soil as the main resource for continuous sustenance of the great population destined to make their homes here."

Surely when the coal and iron age is over, and iron becomes a luxury, there will be some shifting of the methods of mankind. We can grow a few trees perhaps in time where the forests once stood, but we can't make coal deposits and iron ore.

It would appear then there might be some hope of finding tenants for the abandoned farms of New England and New York State within that period, and that dairying and breeding dairy cattle, even Ayrshires, will yet become profitable, if farming is to be the final source of wealth, the one permanent industry to give employment and feed the hordes that will crowd our shores.

Let us hope the Sovereigns of the Soil, the individual farmers of to-day, will cling to their broad acres and teach their children that sterling character, the highest type of citizenship, the strength of the Nation, are developed in country homes, under the trees and in the open fields; and numerous herds and abundant harvests will reward the intelligent toilers of succeeding generations, and help to dignify and perpetuate distinctive family abodes.

If the burden of rearing upon pure and wholesome milk, the babies of that vast population, is to fall upon the four leading dairy breeds in this country, not only must the increase in herds and improvement of dairy conditions keep pace with the people, but the product of the Ayrshire, of all the breeds, being in quality nearest the mother's milk, the natural food for the babe (neither too thin and lean, nor too thick and rich), unlimited demand should be had in every dairy district, for Ayrshire cows, when such advantage has been published and become widely known.

Gentlemen, if this Association was trying to promote and make popular an inferior breed of cattle, without merit, there might be some excuse for its being, of the four Associations representing the four dairy breeds, the one least progressive and prosperous. It has without doubt or question the favorite breed, but the Association is not pursuing proper methods to insure great success and popularity for Ayrshires in the United States.

This Association has neither the money nor the progressive management to compete with the other dairy breeds, in obtaining its just share of public favor and proper prices for its cattle.

Ayrshire registered bulls to-day sell at beef prices with few exceptions; and there is a great work to be done in breeding uniformity of excellence in the cows.

Fortunately the uniform scale of points lately adopted for Ayrshires in Scotland, Canada and the United States by the respective Associations, establishes the one type for utility and beauty to breed up to.

Utility and uniformity in the Ayrshire Cow must be had to compete successfully with the other dairy breeds, and with renewed energy and life in the Association, I believe much higher prices can be established and maintained for Ayrshires of quality.

At the National Dairy Show in Chicago this last fall, there was the greatest display of high bred Ayrshires that ever came together.

It was an object lesson in the West for the Ayrshire breed which will be remembered. I hope some one who witnessed the scene will describe it here to-day. This Association contributed through its Committee $490 for special prizes at that Fair, being the only prize contribution made by the Association during the last year; and thanks to the promptness of the Treasurer, Mr. Winsor, the awards have been paid to each winner.

The Executive Committee met at the New Bingham Hotel, Philadelphia, on November 26th, 1907, and by appointment of sub-committees on Bulls—on Bovine Tuberculosis,—on Judges at Fairs,—on Proxies, etc., began a lot of good work which if sustained by the members here to-day, much progress of the right kind can be made for the Association.

As to the Bulls, I desire to repeat what I said at the last annual meeting: "All bulls without positive indications of milking qualities, should never be put into service. Raise the registration fee to five dollars for every bull, and none but the best would be likely to get into the records." And I will say further that the Committee on Bulls can do great good if given power to act.

As to Bovine Tuberculosis, it deserves your most serious consideration and severe treatment.

Much depends upon these two subjects being wisely and properly handled.

Gentlemen, for two terms, now closing, I have done what I could possibly do, with limited time at my command, to further the best interests of the Association, as its President, without fear or favor; and I desire to thank you for the confidence imposed in me.

The custom shall be preserved that no third term will prevail, therefore its mantle must fall upon other shoulders of your selection to-day, who I trust will have the time and the inclination to inaugurate and carry out such work as will enlarge the scope and usefulness of the Association, and help raise to a higher average, a higher standard, the utility, uniformity and quality of the Ayrshire breed in the United States.

Followed by applause.

Mr. Converse—I move that a vote of thanks of the Association be extended to the President for this most truthful and intelligent address.

Voted unanimously.

The President—The reading of the Minutes of the last meeting is in order.

The Secretary—The Minutes of the last meeting are in the Year Book, copies of which are here for distribution.

Mr. Pember—I move that the reading of the Minutes of the last meeting be dispensed with.

Motion seconded, and carried.

The President—The Secretary will please call the roll.

ROLL CALL

To the call of the roll by the Secretary, the following members responded in person:

Henry Dorrance	Plainfield, Conn.
Wm. Stewart Tod	East Stanwich, Conn.
William T. Wells	Newington, Conn.
Elmer F. Pember	Bangor, Me.
J. N. Abbott	Concord, N. H.
Charles J. Bell	Hollis, N. H.
Etna J. Fletcher	So. Lyndeboro, N. H.
Charles H. Hayes	Portsmouth, N. H.
Strafford County Farm, by F. M. Handy	Dover, N. H.
George H. Yeaton	Dover, N. H.
Joseph F. Burke	Morristown, N. J.
J. Andrew Casterline	Dover, N. J.
William Lindsay	Plainfield, N. J.
J. D. & B. P. Magie	Elizabeth, N. J.
W. V. Probasco	Cream Ridge, N. J.
George William Ballou	Middletown, N. Y.
J. F. Converse	Woodville, N. Y.
Gerald Howatt	White Plains, N. Y.
George E. Pike	Gouverneur, N. Y.
B. C. Sears	Blooming Grove, N. Y.
Oliver Smith & Son	Chateaugay, N. Y.
J. Walter Wood	Clayton, N. Y.
Howard Cook	Beloit, Ohio
J. F. Butterfield	So. Montrose, Pa.
Friends Asylum, by Henry Hall	Philadelphia, Pa.
Hillview Stock Farm, Ltd...by J. H. Dewees,	Paoli, Pa.
B. Luther Shimer	Bethlehem, Pa.

Thomas Turnbull, Jr..................Allegheny, Pa.
John R. Valentine..................Bryn Mawr, Pa.
Nicholas S. Winsor..................Greenville, R. I.
C. M. Winslow........................Brandon, Vt.
L. C. Spalding & Son..................Poultney, Vt.
L. A. Reymann......................Wheeling, W. Va.
W. F. Stephen.....................Huntington, Que.

The following members were represented by proxy:

George Bement........................Fruitvale, Cal.
Ella R. Aiken ....Norwalk, Conn.
John A. Baton & Son..............Wauregan, Conn.
Connecticut Agricultural College........Storrs, Conn.
Alfred A. Ennis..................Danielson, Conn.
George A. Kahn........................Yantic, Conn.
J. H. Larned........................Putnam, Conn.
Edward G. Palmer..................Plainfield, Conn.
N. E. Sears........................Elmwood, Conn.
Dudley Wells, 2d...............Wethersfield, Conn.
Granville Jones ....Galesburgh, Ill.
John Stewart ....Elburn, Ill.
C. C. Richards....................Malotte Park, Ind.
George B. Bearce......................Lewiston, Me.
J. P. Buckley ....Stroudwater, Me.
A. J. Dearborne ....West Falmouth, Me.
Good Will Home Association............Hinckley, Me.
A. A. Hunnewell................New Gloucester, Me.
Charles K. Harrison..................Pikesville, Md.
J. McPherson Scott..................Hagerstown, Md.
P. K. Bacon........................Campello, Mass.
B. F. Barnes........................Haverhill, Mass.
C. M. Beldon ....South Natick, Mass.
Enos W. Boise ....Blandford, Mass.
George H. Bowker..................Westboro, Mass.
Jairus F. Burt....................Easthampton, Mass.
Franklin P. Clark..................Sudbury, Mass.

Davis Copeland & Son................Campello, Mass.
Charles C. Doe.....................Lexington, Mass.
Easterbrook Bros....................Webster, Mass.
C. A. French..................North Andover, Mass.
H. A. Harrington...................Worcester, Mass.
A. M. Haskell...................North Beverly, Mass.
James Lawrence ....Groton, Mass.
J. Hooper Leach..................Bridgewater, Mass.
Philo Leach ....Bridgewater, Mass.
Wm. H. Marsh...................Barre Plains, Mass.
Harry E. Morrell....................Wayland, Mass.
F. C. Peirce................Concord Junction, Mass.
George H. Peirce.....................Concord, Mass.
Anson C. Piper.................South Acton, Mass.
Hammon Reed ....Lexington, Mass.
Charles D. Sage.............North Brookfield, Mass.
Peter D. Smith......................Andover, Mass.
George F. Stone....................Littleton, Mass.
Edmund H. Stevens................Cambridge, Mass.
Thaxter Scott & Son..................Hawley, Mass.
Arthur F. Tyler ....Athol, Mass.
Michigan School for the Deaf............Flint, Mich.
James J. Hill ....St. Paul, Minn.
C. McC. Reeve..................Minneapolis, Minn.
John W. Scott ....Austin, Minn.
John F. Wilcox..................Minneapolis, Minn.
James Surget ....Natchez, Miss.
University of Missouri.................Columbia, Mo.
E. M. Davidson & Son..............Bozeman, Montana
Stephen R. Breck..................Claremont, N. H.
H. F. Cater & Son...........North Barrington, N. H.
Harlow N. Childs...................Piermont, N. H.
George C. Clark......................Orford, N. H.
W. L. Cross.........................Ponemah, N. H.
W. R. Garvin ....Dover, N. H.

Charles S. Hayes..................Portsmouth, N. H.
Andy Holt ....Lyndeboro, N. H.
E. A. Holt ....Hudson, N. H.
William C. Marshall.................Laconia, N. H.
C. E. Rockwood & Son................Temple, N. H.
Frank E. Russell...................Greenfield, N. H.
E. E. Sawyer......................Atkinson, N. H.
Charles H. Upham & Son......Thornton's Ferry, N. H.
The Uplands ....Bridgewater, N. H.
Frederick H. Beach ....Dover, N. J.
F. C. Farley.......................Milburn, N. J.
W. R. Whittingham..................Milburn, N. J.
Arden Farms Dairy Co................Arden, N. Y.
F. M. Babcock ....Gouverneur, N. Y.
C. S. Barney......................Milford, N. Y.
Kent Barney ....Milford, N. Y.
N. Barnes ....Middle Hope, N. Y.
George H. Bell ....Rome, N. Y.
Thomas J. Burdick & Sons..............Alfred, N. Y.
E. L. Button........................Melrose, N. Y.
C. W. Clark ....Guymard, N. Y.
N. E. Clark........................Potsdam, N. Y.
Lawton M. Conger ....Collins, N. Y.
H. W. Cookingham ....Cherry Creek, N. Y.
Elmer J. Dorn ....Johnstown, N. Y.
J. H. Griffin ....Moira, N. Y.
James H. Gurnsey & Co..............Woodhull, N. Y.
Lott Hall ....Gouverneur, N. Y.
Eugene Ham ....Verbank, N. Y.
Wm. Pierson Hamilton.............Sterlington, N. Y.
C. E. Hatch......................Gainesville, N. Y.
H. A. Horton ....Johnson, N. Y.
George D. Hubbard ....Camden, N. Y.
L. Huffstater ....Sandy Creek, N. Y.
S. S. Karr & Sons...................Almond, N. Y.

Louis H. Kenyon ....Utopia, N. Y.
E. Ten Eyck Lansing.............Little Falls, N. Y.
J. S. Leach & Son.................Gouverneur, N. Y.
C. W. Lewis & Sons..............Alfred Station, N. Y.
A. L. Litchard & Son................Rushford, N. Y.
Robert McCrea....................Champlain, N. Y.
W. W. & H. B. Mercereau.............Vestal, N. Y.
James H. Nichols......................Carmel, N. Y.
Ormiston Brothers......................Cuba, N. Y.
T. F. Rhodes........................Camillus, N. Y.
Clarence Ricker......................Belmont, N. Y.
G. L. Rodger ....Gouverneur, N. Y.
Arthur B. Ryder...................Barnerville, N. Y.
E. A. Schouten.....................Cortland, N. Y.
D. E. Siver......................Cooperstown, N. Y.
Francis Lynde Stetson............Sterlington, N. Y.
F. D. & E. Stowell...............Black Creek, N. Y.
W. C. Stowell....................Black Creek, N. Y.
J. P. Strickland ....Cattaraugus, N. Y.
George Taber....................East Aurora, N. Y.
Ambie S. Tubbs.................Maple View, N. Y.
W. G. Tucker....................Elm Valley, N. Y.
M. A. Tuttle....................Hornellsville, N. Y.
C. S. Underhill.....................Glenham, N. Y.
Samuel Verplank....................Fishkill, N. Y.
M. J. Ward.......................Treadwell, N. Y.
M. G. Welch & Son....................Burke, N. Y.
C. P. Whitney......................Orleans, N. Y.
John Will..................Fort Covington, N. Y.
L. W. Whipple & Son................Malone, N. Y.
Henry Betts........................Pittsfield, Ohio
J. H. Crane & Sons....................Toledo, Ohio
D. E. Howatt.......................Cleveland, Ohio
A. B. McConnell & Son ....Wellington, Ohio
A. J. Wilson.........................Grafton, Ohio

J. D. Honeyman.....................Portland, Ore.
H. S. Ayer..........................Columbus, Pa.
O. P. Blakeslee....................Spartansburg, Pa.
Christopher Byrne..................Friendsville, Pa.
Patrick Byrne ....St. Josephs, Pa.
George L. Cass.....................Sunbury, Pa.
A. M. Cornell.........................Altus, Pa.
W. E. Farrell ....Corry, Pa.
Willis W. Hopkins..................Aldenville, Pa.
C. F. McCray & Son.................Corry, Pa.
George H. McFadden................Bryn Mawr, Pa.
R. J. Munce.......................Washington, Pa.
John W. Oakey....................Bryn Mawr, Pa.
C. L. Peck ....Coudersport, Pa.
Percival Roberts, Jr..................Narberth, Pa.
John Simpson........................Scranton, Pa.
C. E. Stewart.......................Hartstown, Pa.
Robert Templeton & Son..................Ulster, Pa.
Edward S. Bowen..................Pawtucket, R. I.
Estate of Obadiah Brown...........Providence, R. I.
H. S. Joslin........................Mohegan, R. I.
Everett P. Sherman................Harrisville, R. I.
Leander Sherman..................Harrisville, R. I.
Benjamin F. Smith..............North Scituate, R. I.
Daniel A. Smith......................Tarkiln, R. I.
S. Frank Tefft.....................Hamilton, R. I.
William P. Vaughn.................Providence, R. I.
W. G. Hinson.....................Charleston, S. C.
H. C. Groome......................Warrenton, Va.
A. R. Venable, Jr..................Farmville, Va.
C. A. Abell.......................St. Albans, Vt.
A. J. Anderson & Son............No. Craftsbury, Vt.
C. W. Buck.......................Brownsville, Vt.
B. F. Butterfield ....Derby Line, Vt.
H. A. Clark........................Hyde Park, Vt.

F. A. Drew....................So. Burlington, Vt.
George Dunsmore......................Swanton, Vt.
Charles W. Emerson..................Charlotte, Vt.
Fisher & May.................St. Albans Hill, Vt.
A. M. Fletcher....................Proctorsville, Vt.
Forest Park Farm.....................Brandon, Vt.
J. Barron Foss......................St. Albans, Vt.
Matthew Hannah...................Brownsville, Vt.
W. W. Houghton...................Lyndonville, Vt.
W. H. Jackman......................Vergennes, Vt.
F. A. Joslyn.......................Northfield, Vt.
Lovejoy & Eddy.........................Stowe, Vt.
W. A. Merriam.........................Glover, Vt.
W. C. Nye..........................East Barre, Vt.
R. Parker & Son....................Ferrisburg, Vt.
Fletcher D. Proctor....................Proctor, Vt.
George L. Rice.......................Rutland, Vt.
Charles Sanford......................Ludlow, Vt.
W. F. Scott.........................Brandon, Vt.
G. S. Scribner's Estate ....Castleton, Vt.
C. B. Stevens...................St. Johnsbury, Vt.
Wm. Stanford Stevens...............St. Albans, Vt.
Walter D. Turner...................Moretown, Vt.
Vt. Experiment Station..............Burlington, Vt.
Vermont Industrial School...........Vergennes, Vt.
H. R. C. Watson.....................Brandon, Vt.
Sam Jones...........................Juneau, Wis.
Adam Seitz ....Waukesha, Wis
Fred Tschudy ....Monroe, Wis.
R. R. Ness...........................Howick, Que.

The President—We will now hear the Report of the Secretary.

REPORT OF SECRETARY

The past year has in many respects been the most successful one for Ayrshire interests that we have had for many years.

We have added 31 new members since last meeting.

We have already gone beyond the limit in size for the volumes of the Herd Book, and must close the 19th Volume as soon as February 1st.

The entries to our Herd Book are increasing so rapidly that we must issue a volume annually, in order to keep the size within reasonable limits. We have in volume 19 shortened the description as much as possible consistent with giving a description that would identify an animal. This we did in order to keep the size of the volume as small as possible.

The entries in the Home Dairy Test have increased materially the past year, so much so that they are a prominent feature of the work of the Association.

It seems to your Secretary that some changes in the rules governing the tests might be made to advantage.

The Department at Washington has instituted a set of rules and regulations governing admission to advanced registry for all breeds on a uniform basis, which in its simplicity has advantages which we might adopt to advantage.

Your Secretary has found considerable difficulty in getting proper samples of milk sent to the different Stations, due to carelessness, and to its being left to hired help to take the samples.

Government proposes to send a man to the stable monthly to take the samples, thereby getting more uniform samples.

It seems to your Secretary that the expense of testing should be borne in part by the person having the test made, and not expect the Association to bear all the expense.

The exhibitions at fairs the past year have been unusually attractive and have drawn a good deal of attention to the breed.

There has been an unusual inquiry for information about the breed, coming from all over the country, also there has been an increased call for Ayrshire cattle both from wealthy seekers, and from the common dairymen, which has given a greatly increased addition to the transfers of Ayrshire cattle.

There have been several public sales of Ayrshires, the prices of which have varied greatly, some being phenomenally high, as at the Dairy Show where Denty 9th of Auchenbrain was sold for $1,155. At some other sales the prices were not as satisfactory.

There are so many contingencies hovering around an auction sale that we cannot take the sales as any criterion from which to form an opinion either as to the popular demand for the breed, or the prices which they should bring.

The real index of the demand, and the prices is found in the private sales made by breeders, which I believe has been satisfactory during the past year.

There have been a number of deaths reported during the past year, though not all of them occurred during the year.

William Sellers, Edgemoor, Del.; Judge H. W. Blodgett, Waukegan, Ill.; J. N. Coldren, Iowa City, Iowa; A. A. Adams, Berryton, Kansas; H. Stowits, Abilene, Kan.; George A. Fletcher, Milton, Mass.; John C. Thorp, Holyoke, Mass.; Edward W. Sadler, Montclair, N. J.; Henry E. Seaver, Canton, N. Y.; L. D. Davis, Newport,

R. I.; A. P. Ball, Derby Line, Vt.; Lawrence Brainard, St. Albans, Vt.; L. S. Drew, South Burlington, Vt.; G. S. Scribner, Castleton, Vt.; Chester Hazen, Brandon, Wis.; Joseph Johnson, Hartland, Wis.; Andrew Allan, Montreal, Que.; Obadiah Brown, Providence, R. I.; John W. Burnett, Salem, N. Y.; C. N. Healey, Exeter, N. H.; Chas. R. Milliken, Portland, Me.

It was voted that the Report of the Secretary be accepted and placed on file.

THE PRESIDENT—We will now hear the Financial Report of the Secretary from October 1st, 1906 to January 1st, 1908.

FINANCIAL REPORT OF SECRETARY

From Oct. 1, 1906, to Jan'y 1, 1908.

Rec'd for Entries to members	$1,857 36
" " Entries to non-members	757 25
" " Transfers to members	122 50
" " Transfer to non-members	79 75
" " Customs certificates	10 50
" " Duplicate certificates	7 00
" " Advertisements in Year Book	54 00
" " Pedigree blanks	75
" " Private Herd Books	13 50
" " Milk Record blanks	5 27
" " Examining Canada Herd Book	2 00
" " Volume XVII	4 50
" " Booklets	3 00
" " New members 31	775 00
	$3,692 38

New Members:

      C. W. BUCK.
      BENJ. F. SMITH.
      B. F. BUTTERFIELD.
      C. B. STEVENS.
      CHARLES D. FREEMAN.
      JOHN SIMPSON.
      LOVEJOY & EDDY.
      W. F. STEPHEN.
      W. L. CROSS.
      ELLA R. AIKEN.
      J. J. DELANEY.
      GLEN ALPINE FARM.
      THOMAS J. CROWLEY.
      A. E. HILLMAN & SON.
      GEO. W. BURDICK.
      M. COSGROVE.
      JOHN A. & ROWLAND NESS.
      A. J. ANDERSON & SON.
      ROBT. HUNTER & SON.
      J. S. GREENAWALT.
      EDWARD P. DAVIS.
      THE UPLANDS.
      WM H. FISHER.
      EDMUND H. STEVENS.
      W. S. CRAMTON.
      M. M. BURNHAM.
      E. A. TILTON.
      L. W. WHIPPLE & SON.
      KENT BARENY.
      EASTERBROOK BROS.
      JOHN W. OAKEY.

Approved: Geo. H. Yeaton, Auditor, Jan. 9, 1908.

Money paid out:

Paid for postage	$165 93
Paid for express and freight	25 94
Paid for telephone and telegraph	11 22
Brandon Pub. Co., for printing	126 75
Argus Co., for printing Year Book	273 00
Woodruff for printing slips	1 00
Tuttle Co., binding Herd Books	85 40
Fuller for printing photographs	4 00
Empire Engraving Co., for half-tones	44 17
Photographs at Dairy Show, Chicago	6 75
Eimer Co., for bottles	9 60
Stenographer at annual meeting	44 13
Banquet at Philadelphia	45 00
Am. Surety Co., bond for Treasurer	20 00
Corporation tax	10 00
Use of room at Philadelphia for Ex. Com.	2 00
Office supplies as per bill	10 25
Advertisement Country Gentleman	100 00
Advertisement Hoard's Dairyman	100 00
Committee travel as per bill	245 42
Secretary's salary	700 00
Secretary's travel and expense	88 85
Home Dairy Test, McFadden	95 00
Home Dairy Test, Valentine	80 00
Home Dairy Test, J. G. Clark	35 00
Vermont Dairy Test	49 89
Washington Experiment Station	120 45
New Hampshire Experiment Station	22 80
Massachusetts Experiment Station	65 50
Ohio Experiment Station	10 10
Pennsylvania Experiment Station	86 10
New York Experiment Station	7 38
Connecticut Experiment Station	1 00
	$2,692 63
Check to N. S. Winsor	999 75
	$3,692 38

Dover, N. H., Jan. 9th, 1908.

This certifies that I have examined the books of C. M. Winslow, Secretary of the Ayrshire Breeders' Association. and find them correctly balanced and all payments properly vouched.

GEORGE H. YEATON,
Auditor.

Voted that the Report be accepted and placed on file.

THE PRESIDENT—We will now hear the Report of the Treasurer.

Dover, N. H., Jan. 7, 1908.

This certifies that I have examined the account of N. S. Winsor, Treasurer of the Ayrshire Breeders' Association, for the period from Oct. 1st, 1906, to Dec. 31st, 1907, and found:

Balance on hand Oct. 1st, 1906....	$3,754 15
Nov. dividend, 1906	65 60
May dividend, 1907................	66 90
Nov. dividend, 1907................	57 28
Cash from L. A. Reymann.........	100 00
Cash from C. M. Winslow..........	999 75
Cash from sale of books............	116 00
Total receipts including balance	———$5,159 68

Payments as per vouchers:

Paid N. S. Winsor, expenses at annual meeeting, 1906..............	21 00
Insurance on books................	13 50
G. H. Yeaton, expenses as Auditor...	14 03
Paid freight on books..............	5 70
Paid for stamps	5 84
Argus Co., printing Vol. XVII......	530 00
Argus Co., printing Vol. XVIII....	547 80

Prizes National Dairy Show:

R. R. Ness	$160 00
W. P. Schanck	160 00
Robert Hunter and Son	70 00
G. H. McFadden	45 00
Hillview Stock Farm	5 00
R. H. Mason	50 00

Cash payments $1,627 87

Balance in Treasurer's hands Jan. 1st. 1908..$3,531 81

Of the above amount there is a deposit in
Smithfield Savings Bank.................$2,432 06
Cash in hand............................ 1,119 85

$3,531 81

French Fund, Rutland, Vt., Savings Bank.... 1,607 77

$5,159 68

GEORGE H. YEATON,
Auditor.

Moved and seconded that the Treasurer's Report be accepted and placed on file.

Carried

THE PRESIDENT—The Report of the Finance Committee is next in order.

INVENTORY IN OFFICE OF SECRETARY, DECEMBER 31, 1907.

1 index card and letter case	$50 00
1 writing desk and typewriter combined	45 00
2 typewriters	100 00

1 letter copy machine and desk............	$35 00
1 Burroughs adding machine..............	250 00
157 Private Herd Books...................	157 00
Postage stamps on hand....................	3 37
30 volumes Scotch Herd Books............	30 00
16 volumes Canada Herd Books...........	16 00
4 volumes Bagg Herd Books..............	4 00
4 volumes Sturtevant Herd Books.........	4 00
Usual supply of stationery and blanks......	....
	$694 37

INVENTORY OF BOOKS IN HANDS OF TREASURER Jan. 1st, 1908.

	Need Rebinding.	Good Condition.
Vol. 1		152
Vol. 2 (Old Edition)		2
Vol. 2 (Revised Edition)		94
Vol. 3		87
Vol. 4	3	116
Vol. 5	5	16
Vol. 6		185
Vol. 7		187
Vol. 8		195
Vol. 9 ⎫ Volumes 9. 10 and 11		241
Vol. 10 ⎬ were in folio last year		217
Vol. 11 ⎭ and are now bound into books		212
Vol. 12		223
Vol. 13	1	231
Vol. 14		226
Vol. 15		242

```
Vol. 16 ......................          250
Vol  17 ......................          196
Vol. 18 ......................          277
                                  ─────   ─────
                                      9   3,349
```

3,349 Volumes at $2 00 each...............$6,698 00
   9 Volumes at $1 00 each................   9 00

Total value of volumes...................$6,707 00

It was moved and seconded that the report be accepted and placed on file.

Carried.

THE PRESIDENT—The Report of the Home Dairy Test Committee will now be heard.

REPORT OF THE
HOME DAIRY TEST COMMITTEE FOR THE YEAR
From April, 1906, to April, 1907.

There were some 150 cows started in the test beginning April, 1906, and 86 cows pulled through to April 1, 1907.

The five best cows from each herd stood as follows, on a butter basis:

Geo. H. McFadden, best five for butter.

Lizzie of Barclay..........	8,583 milk	463.40 butter
Auchenbrain Princess 7th..	8,307 milk	405.11 butter
Broomhill Minnie 10th....	8,377 milk	389.46 butter
Queen of Barclay........	8,336 milk	384 24 butter
Jane of Bryn Mawr......	7,301 milk	381.82 butter
	40,904	2,024.03

Geo. H. McFadden after taking out best cow for butter:

Auchenbrain Princess 7th..	8,307	405.11
Broomhill Minnie 10th.....	8,377	389.46
Queen of Barclay..........	8,336	384.24
Jane of Bryn Mawr........	7,301	381.82
Daisy of Rosemont........	8,709	375.35
	41,030	1,935.98

Geo. H McFadden after leaving out the two best cows for butter.

Broomhill Minnie 10th.....	8,377	389.46
Queen of Barclay..........	8,336	384.24
Jane of Bryn Mawr........	7,301	381.82
Daisy of Rosemont........	8,709	375.35
Letta Lind of Radnor......	7,139	373.06
	39,862	1,903.93

E. J. Fletcher best five cows on a butter basis.

Durtharlynne	10,345 milk	438.11 butter
Durwood	9,364 milk	415.10 butter
Queen Lill 2d.............	8,762 milk	367.66 butter
Lady Redwood...........	7,875 milk	323 80 butter
Durwood's Rose...........	7,230 milk	315.06 butter
	43,576	1,859.73

E. J. Fletcher after taking out best cow on a butter basis.

Durwood	9,364	415.10
Queen Lill 2d.............	8,762	367.66

Lady Redwood	7,875	323.80
Durwood's Rose	7,230	315.06
Rose Mona	6,925	300.43
	40,156	1,722.05

J. F. Butterfield best five cows on a butter basis.

Ada Rome	9,045	374.27
Angeline Sebastian	7,406	351.58
Agnese Sebastian	7,619	331.83
Ida Webb	7,229	327.68
Phoebe Webb	7,836	316.87
	39,135	1,702.23

C. M. Winslow & Son best five cows on a butter basis.

Acelista	9,794 milk	396.13 butter
Claud M.	6,133 milk	327.08 butter
Olive Kilbowie	6,924 milk	320.87 butter
Juliette C.	6,640 milk	319.27 butter
Myrtle Kilbowie	6,882 milk	315.40 butter
	36,373	1,678.75

Geo. H. Yeaton best five cows on a butter basis.

Miss Olga	8,118	387.10
Ponemah	6,996	334.15
Uarda	7,916	328.92
Ouilma	7,946	311.71
Maumee	7,751	311.48
	38,727	1,673.36

A. B. McConnell & Son best five cows on a butter basis.

Clarissa Loraine	9,051	383.68
Mary A. M. 2d	9,132	371.61
Miss Edna	6,804	311.43
Ida Douglas	5,972	294.44
Sahara	6,154	284.36
	37,113	1,645.52

L. C. Spalding & Son best five cows on a butter basis.

Lillian Drummond 4th	8,311	365.79
Brooklawn Acme	6,900	277.57
Miss Acme Douglas	6,479	274.88
Rose Morning	6,451	255.61
Major Acme's Myra	5,359	239.13
	33,500	1,412.98

L. A. Reymann did not have cows enough to compete as a herd.

The awards offered were for three single cows in the Home Dairy Test, a single cow for the Country Gentleman Cup.

Three Herd Prizes in the Home Dairy Test, and the French prize silver cup.

Your Committee made the awards as follows, selecting the best cows for the single cow prizes, those in the three prizes in the Home Dairy Test being on a butter basis, and the Country Gentleman Cup on a basis of both milk and butter.

First prize for single cow to Geo. H. McFadden for
Lizzie of Barclay 8,583 lbs. of milk and 463.40 lbs. butter.

Second prize for single cow to L. A. Reymann for

Madonna Lass 2d, 9,785 lbs. milk, 438.82 lbs. butter.

Third prize to Geo. H. McFadden for

Auchenbrain Princess 7th, 8,307 lbs. milk and 405.11 lbs. butter.

The Country Gentleman Silver Cup was awarded on a basis of both milk and butter on a scale of points, to

E. J. Fletcher for

Durtharlynne, 10,345 lbs. of milk, 438.11 lbs. butter, scaling 16,917 points

The awards for herds in the Home Dairy Test were as follows:

E. J. Fletcher, herd of five cows, giving 40,156 lbs. of milk, 1,722.05 lbs. butter.

Dr. J. F. Butterfield, 2d.. 39,135   1,702.23

C. M. Winslow, 3d...... 36,373   1,678.75

The French prize for a silver cup for best five cows on a basis of both milk and butter was awarded to Geo. H. McFadden, on herd giving 39,862 lbs. milk and 1,903.93 lbs. butter.

There are entered and being tested for the year 1907-8 about 200 cows.

FOR ADVANCED REGISTRY AND THE HOME DAIRY TEST.

Entered by:

Geo. H. McFadden, John R. Valentine, Percival Roberts Jr., Dr. J. F. Butterfield, J. W. Clise, Geo. F. Stone,

Geo. H. Yeaton, E. J. Fletcher, L. C. Spalding & Son, C. M. Winslow, Henry Dorrance, Matthew Hannah, L. A. Reymann, Hillview Stock Farm, S. S. Karr & Sons.

All of which is respectfully submitted.

C. M. WINSLOW,
THOS. TURNBULL Jr.,
GEO. WM. BALLOU,
WM. T. WELLS,
Home Dairy Test Committee.

Voted that the Report be accepted and placed on file.

THE PRESIDENT—We will now hear the Report of the Advanced Registry Committee.

THE SECRETARY—It was recommended by the Executive Committee that the Association adopt a standard of its own, and conform as far as possible to the Government standard, and that we have a double standard.

MR. VALENTINE—That is, that we do not abolish our own system of Advanced Registry tests. It was recommended that it be submitted to the meeting this afternoon whether they should recommend that the Government standard be adopted for the Ayrshire Breeders' Association tests, thereby eliminating our own Advanced Registry test. The Committee felt it was better to recommend that the Advanced Registry tests of the Ayrshire Breeders' Association be continued, and in addition to our own go into the Government test if we desire.

I make the motion that two standards be adopted, and that the Advanced Registry tests as adopted by the Ayrshire Breeders' Association be continued.

MR. OAKEY—I would like to know whether that motion includes the same figures that we have been testing by, or if the Executive Committee recommend a raise.

THE PRESIDENT—That is the principle involved. It is a question whether we have these two standards. Now the motion is on having the two standards, the Government and our own. Now for the question.

MR. PIKE—Are the figures already settled in the Government standard?

THE SECRETARY—The Government standard is a higher standard than the one we have adopted. We proposed to call the two-year-old cow standard 6,000 lbs. of milk; the Government places it at 6,500. We proposed to raise our butter standard on a ratio of 25 lbs. of butter, or its equivalent in butter fat to make the equivalent of a 25 lb. addition along up through the different grades.

MR. REYMANN—I was present this morning when this proposition was being discussed, and I also had the pleasure of speaking concerning it with Mr. Winslow at a former date, and I believe we have considered the proposition carefully. But for the benefit of those who may not have considered it, I would like to say that this is my idea of the proposition: That we recognize a double standard; in other words, a cow that we desire to place in the Advanced Registry must live up to and conform with a two-fold standard, viz., a minimum of milk production and a minimum of butter production within a certain given time, viz., a year for the yearly test or a week for the weekly test. The Government standard, of course, was made for the purpose of covering all breeds of cattle, particularly the special purpose or dairy breeds, the Jersey, Guernsey, Holstein, Ayrshire and others—by reason of the fact that some of these breeds give a large quantity of milk and a small percentage of butter fat and others give a large amount of butter fat in a year with relatively a small amount of milk in comparison. Therefore they tried to fix a standard for the milk end of it and for the butter end of it, so that all the breeds could come within this standard of merit.

Now, it would raise the mature cows; as Mr. Winslow has explained to you, the minimum is 10,000 lbs. of milk,—that is for a milk standard. She is then considered a milk standard cow Advanced Registry. Officially tested by the Government at 10,000 lbs. she is practically a Government Advanced Registry milch cow. Giving 420 lbs. of butter, she is a Government Advanced Registry butter cow; but she may be either without being both. Now what we propose to do is to continue our Advanced Registry, making neither one of these as high as the minimum required in either instance by the Government, but require that each animal shall conform to both minimums. In other words, the Government says if a cow gives 10,000 lbs. of milk she is entitled to Advanced Registry as a milk-giving animal. Now we have required both of those things—a milk standard and a butter standard. It was proposed this morning to raise each one of those all along the line, beginning with the two-year-olds and extending up to the aged class. And after considering it from all points of view I believe it is best to continue our Advanced Registry, and we can run this Government test along with it and gain the full benefit.

Mr. Valentine—The question is before you for a vote

Motion seconded and carried.

The President—Now comes the question of each Article or Rule being adopted as we go along.

RULES FOR ADVANCED REGISTRY

(Secretary reads Preamble, Rule I).

The President—It is proposed, as we go along, if you find no objection, that we adopt the rules as read one by one. There are some things you may think have been overlooked, but I think you will find when you get through that everything has been considered.

Dr. Turnbull—I move that we adopt Rule I.

Motion seconded and carried.

The Secretary—(Reads Rule II).

Mr. Bell—I move that the clause in Rule II referring to the weekly test be stricken out, and that a cow be only entitled to Advanced Registry that has completed a full year's record.

Motion seconded and carried.

The Secretary—It seems to me, gentlemen, that the seven-day test might remain. The whole expense is borne by the individual owning the cow and having the test made. A seven-day test does no harm to the Association and costs nothing, and it seems to me it is a good thing to have this test made.

Mr. Bell—Out of a herd of 26 cows, the cow that gave the most milk in one week gave the least milk in the whole year of the whole 26. Now that cow has paid her keeping for a year, still on your seven-day test she might be in the Advanced Registry, and I do not think she is entitled to it.

The Secretary—(Reads Rule III).

Moved to adopt as it stands, seconded and carried.

The Secretary—(Reads Rule IV).

Mr. VALENTINE—I would like to move that that be amended so as to strike out all "scaling"; that a bull shall be admitted to Advanced Registry on having four daughters in Advanced Registry.

Mr. OAKEY—I would like to add to that amendment that he have four daughters from different dams.

Mr. VALENTINE—I accept that amendment.

Dr. BUTTERFIELD—I do not know if this is all right but I look at it from a different standpoint from anything that has been said. While a number of us have some animals in the Advanced Registry, this move leaves those animals in the Advanced Registry, but puts a bar upon others who might get in who have as good animals as they are. In a word, it makes a "trust" on the business, and I do not know if a move in that direction is just right.

Mr. SEARS—Don't you throw away the value if you don't make him scale in points? It seems to me that a bull, being the head of a herd, should show well at fairs, though some very homely bulls get very good calves—I think the breed is entitled to be reflected in the bull.

Mr. DORRANCE—I think we ought not to throw away the scaling of points.

Mr. WELLS—I agree with Mr. Dorrance. One thing that has been overlooked is the idea that we cannot scale a bull after he is dead. These daughters usually come up for registry after the bulls are dead.

THE SECRETARY—That question came up last season. Mr. Reymann had a bull that had sired several heifers, but the bull was dead. He sent a photograph of the animal and your Secretary with Mr Reymann's information concluded that that bull would scale 80 points.

We judged from the photograph, and our recollection of the looks of the bull.

Mr. Valentine—If there is any objection to it, why not leave the Rule as it is—that the bull can have two daughters in the Advanced Registry and scale 80 points, and if he has four daughters that proved eligible for Advanced Registry, need not be scaled. I withdraw my resolution.

Mr. Pike—I suggest that Mr. Valentine insert his clause regarding the two daughters being from different dams.

Mr. Stephens (Secretary of the Canadian Ayrshire Breeders' Association)—I do not wish to say very much regarding your rules here, but I would like to say that our rules for Advanced Registry, as well as our scale of points, harmonize with the American, and even the Scotch—allow me to read our standard for registry:

"CANADIAN AYRSHIRE RECORD OF PERFORMANCE.

STANDARD FOR REGISTRATION.

Bulls—Admitted after having four daughters in the Record of Performance, each from a different dam.

Cows—Admitted after fulfilling the following requirements of production and breeding as supervised by the Live Stock Branch of the Department of Agriculture.

All cows admitted must equal or exceed both the records specified below:

	Lbs. Milk.	Lbs. Butter Fat.
Two-year-old class	5,500	198
Three-year-old class	6,500	234

Four-year-old class....	7,500	270
Mature class..........	8,500	306

The per cent. of butter fat shall be determined by Babcock test.

YEAR'S MILE RECORD.

If the test be commenced the day the animal is two years old, or previous to that day, she must produce within 365 consecutive days from that date, 5,500 pounds of milk. For each day the animal is over two years old at the beginning of her year's test, the amount of milk she will be required to produce in the year will be determined by adding 2.75 lbs. for every such day to the 5,500 lbs. required when in the two-year-old class. This ratio is applicable until the animal is five years old, when the required amount will have reached 8,500 lbs., which will be the minimum amount of milk required of all cows five years old or over.

YEAR'S BUTTER FAT RECORD.

If test be commenced the day the animal is two years old, or previous to that day, she must produce within 365 consecutive days from that date, 198 lbs. of butter fat. For each day the animal is over two years old at the beginning of her year's test, the amount of butter fat she will be required to produce in one year will be determined by adding .1 (one tenth) of a pound for each such day to the 218 lbs. required when in the two-year-old class. This ratio is applicable until the animal is five years old when the required amount will have reached 306 lbs., which will be the minimum amount of butter fat required of all cows five years old and over.

Every cow accepted for registration of production must drop a calf within fifteen months after the commencement of the test. In the 4-year-old class and the mature class, no cow will be accepted for registration of production if the beginning of her previous lactation period was more than fifteen months before the commencement of test.

All applications to be addressed to W. F. Stephen, Huntingdon, Quebec, Secretary of the Canadian Ayrshire Breeders' Association.''

This gentleman has made a point. We take into consideration that in nine cases out of ten a bull is dead before his daughters come into the Advanced Registry.

Mr. Valentine—My reason for making the suggestion was that it is such a difficult thing to get anybody to give a scale. The bull is dead, or else he has four daughters and he did not need to be scaled. But I am perfectly willing to withdraw my motion and accept Mr. Oakey's suggestion that it be made two or four daughters from different dams, and that the rest stand as it is.

The President—The amendment as proposed by Mr. Oakey that it should be "two daughters" or "four daughters"—as I understand you wish to amend it so that it reads, "two daughters," or "four daughters without scaling."

Motion put and carried.

The Secretary—(Reads Rule V, Section B, Year's Record)—The increase recommended was to increase the milk 500 lbs. and the equivalent of 25 lbs. of butter, in each class.

Mr. Oakey—In regard to the raise in our Advanced Registry class, I think it would probably be all right to raise it in the three-year-old form, but considering my experience in the last three years I think we will be asking too much to raise our four-year-old and aged cow standard. If we have to force our best cows so that we ruin them or use them up, we are not accomplishing what we want to accomplish. Another thing, we have a lot of cows now entered for Advanced Registry, and if we raise this standard we form a "trust" on those who have their cows in the Advanced Registry. And I think when you get a cow that will qualify with the year's record of 8,500 lbs. of milk and 375 lbs. of butter, you have a good cow; and we should be satisfied with a cow that will do that and bring us a good strong calf every year and not try to force them to the verge of ruin. Those who want to go into the Government test of course can do so, but all breeders, I think, after they have tested this thing for three years, as I have, will think twice before they try to get 10,000 lbs. of milk and 420 lbs. of butter out of a cow.

Mr. Reymann—I agree with Mr. Oakey in what he says in respect to the tests that are now going on. I do not think it would be right or proper to raise the standard while a man is testing his cow, and take it for granted that this will not be applied to those animals who are in the test now but should only apply to those who start it in the future. I disagree with Mr. Oakey on the other proposition. This is primarily an Advanced Registry, it is a Registry of Merit, and it is not every cow that can get in, and if every cow got into the Advanced Registry, there would be no occasion for it. It should be a Registry in which only the most phenomenal cows of the breed are entitled to be recorded. We are raising the standard, it is true. I do not know that I am particularly in favor of it, because I have had considerable trouble making the Advanced Registry without this raise. Still, I propose to try and see if I cannot raise the standard of my cattle to conform with this raise. I will try for more production, and I think we can get it. If the other breeders get it, why should not we. We are just in the infancy of this Advanced Registry and we have not had enough of it to know we can produce greater records, and I am sure in the future it will be far easier to approach the present standard than when this Advanced Registry system was instituted. Therefore, I am in favor of making this raise in the requirements both as to milk and butter fat.

Mr. Valentine—I have a good deal of experience in this matter of testing cattle for the Advanced Registry, perhaps as much as any breeder here, and I must say that looking over the past, I think it would be a mistake as long as we have the two standards already,—milk and butter—to raise the four-year-old and the mature cows. As far as our experience goes there is no trouble at all in classifying the two-year-olds; and there is no trouble in classifying the three-year-olds; but when you come to the mature cow you have a very different proposition,—that has been our experience. Therefore, just to get the question before the meeting I am going to propose that the amendments as read by the Secretary be accepted, with the further amendment that the standards in regard to the four-year-old and the mature forms shall be left as they are at present.

Dr. Butterfield—I second that motion. I think if you raise the standard to the extent we are talking of, it will frighten away many who have planned to put their cattle in the Advanced Registry, but if you raise the standard they won't dare to try.

The President—Then the motion is to accept the increased amount, which in the two-year-old is 6,000 lbs. milk and 250 lbs. or its equivalent of butter fat; 7,000 lbs. milk in the three-year-old form and 300 lbs. of butter; and the other forms, the four-year-old and the mature forms to remain as they are now in the book.

Mr. Reymann—I fear you will get into difficulty. It will not figure out.

Mr. Wells—From the amendment for 6,000 for a two-year-old to 8,500 in the case of the three and four-year-old, makes the figures in proportion.

Mr. Valentine—I do not see what the difficulty is that Mr. Reymann alludes to.

Mr. Reymann—With respect to the additional requirements for animals that are more than three-years old. Figure out these requirements with respect to three-year-olds and if you change the basis on which this whole system is founded or change it to the three-year-olds, and let the four-year-olds remain, you will get into difficulty, because it does not figure out uniformly.

Mr. Valentine—If you make this apply to the three-year and four-year-old class, and let the mature cows remain as they are, you would not meet with that difficulty.

Mr. Fletcher—You could fix your two-year-old form and then graduate it up to the mature cow.

The Secretary—It would not be absolutely uniform. It would be a little hard on the four-year-old possibly; it would favor the three-year-old, but it would figure a scale along up both in milk and butter, and would figure out as between the 6,000 and the 8,500 easily.

Mr. Reymann—You might fix it as definite for the four-year-old, as well as for the five-year-old, and not have it graduated.

The Secretary—Then you would have to figure out a standard for the days.

Mr. Reymann—Not for the four-year-olds, because it stops right there.

The Secretary—Suppose a cow is four-years-old and 364 days,—it is giving her great advantage.

Mr. Reymann—I am suggesting this as a way out.

Mr. Fletcher—To get at the matter, I would like to make an amendment to the motion that we make this two-year-old form 6,000 lbs. of milk and 250 lbs. of butter, leave the mature cow of five years where it is at the present time, and the three and four-year-old be graduated between the two.

The President—That has been Mr. Valentine's motion as amended, and he has accepted the amendment.

Motion put and carried.

The Secretary (Reads Rule VI)—Moved and seconded that the Rule be adopted as read.

Carried.

The Secretary (Reads Rule VII)—Moved and seconded that the Rule be adopted as read.

Carried.

The Secretary—(Reads Rule VIII).

The President—This Rule is now recommended by the Executive Committee as read. The Secretary will please also read Rule IX as bearing on Rule VIII as just read and recommended by the Executive Committee.

(Secretary reads Rule IX).

Moved and seconded to accept and adopt Rules VIII and IX as read.

Carried.

The Secretary—(Reads Rule X).

Voted to accept Rule X.

The Secretary—(Reads Rule XI).

Voted to accept Rule XI.

Mr. Valentine—Was it not recommended that the standard be changed from "butter" to "butter fat?"

The President—Yes, that appears all the way through.

Mr. Valentine—It is called to my attention that we did not adopt any percentage. Now the Holstein people have 80%, and Jersey and Guernsey 85%. I think we ought to set our standard.

The Secretary—I move that we set a standard to conform to the Experiment Station standard.

Motion seconded and carried.

The President—There are Committees to report. We will now hear the report of the Committee on Bulls.

Mr. Reymann—The Committee on Bulls, of which I was a member, have no written report to make. Our Committee was to bring this matter before the Association for discussion. To give a few words of history in this matter: The Executive Committee at its last meeting in November decided that the attention of all breeders of Ayrshire cattle should be called to the fact that many are keeping within their herds animals that are hardly fit to reproduce themselves. We had no particular man in mind, and the still more lamentable proposition occurred to us that most of the animals who have proven themselves great sires, by the time they have come to the attention of the public, have been disposed of, and have been lost to the Ayrshire world,—perhaps killed, or lost sight of. Furthermore, it seemed to us that a great many animals, bulls of superior individuality, were practically unsalable, because of the fact that they had reached a certain age. In the other associations it is the old animal, the tried animal, that is the prize. In the Ayrshire breed, I am sorry to say that the contrary has been true. Look at the public sales,—reflect upon what was bid at the sale in Chicago for an old Ayrshire bull advertized to be still in his prime, and who had proven his worth as a sire. Now, what we want if possible is to encourage the keeping of the valuable sire, and discourage the raising of animals that are not proper animals to keep in a thoroughbred dairy herd. And the first step is to raise the registry fee from $1.00 and $2.00 to $5.00 and $10.00. This was discussed at the last meeting and I think some action should be taken to decide with respect to this proposition, and hope it will be the sense of this meeting to do so. There are other propositions: In the Island of Jersey, as I understand it, a male is not eligible for registry before he has reached a certain age.

Mr. Valentine—When a bull calf is dropped, the Secretary of the Association is notified, and certifies to the birth of the calf. I think the age for registry is six months. Probably Mr. Fuller is more familiar with that than I am.

Mr. Fuller—My recollection is not that the bull has to come up for examination, but the female, as the female must be entered for registry before she is nine months of age. Then she is never brought up for examination until she is milked. As to the male, I am not sure as to the age, but his mother must come, unless she has been scored or has died or has left the Island. And the scale of points recommends that the scale shall increase or decrease according to the points the mother has made.

Mr. Valentine—She must be exhibited with him unless she has scored before, or is dead, or has left the Island.

Mr. Reymann—Of course that proposition would be a very severe one. It is entirely impractical for us to follow. A breeder never knows when a bull calf is born whether he is going to be a good animal at six and a half months, and very often he keeps an animal until it is three months old and then butchers it. Now, our recommendation is not to register animals until they are three months old, so that the breeder can satisfy himself that the animal is a worthy one to be registered, because if he pays $5.00 or $10.00 he wants to feel sure it is going to be a worthy animal after three months of age. So we recommend that no bull calf be registered until he is three months old, and that the breeder certify that the animal is a typical one and comes from a typical sire and dam.

Mr. VALENTINE—That would stop the sale of bulls under three months.

Mr. REYMANN—I think Mr. Valentine would say this was best. He doubtless has many cows whose calves he would feel certain as turning out all right; I have had some that looked pretty good to me at one stage of the game but later on they disappointed me. Those are the recommendations of the Committee, and I only regret that we have no written report to offer. We merely recommend these things in order to bring them up for discussion, and it is such an important preposition, I hope you will all give us your views.

Mr. CASTERLINE—I trust this action will not be taken. I have been a judge in the show rings of the different Agricultural Societies for 30 to 35 years, and I am willing to confess that at three months,—the limit fixed by our member—no judge can determine the value of a bull any more than he can as a young calf. The making of a bull is beyond that age. I would like to see every bull calf bred by a member of this Association registered, the registry fee not to be higher than it is now. I do not believe it is wise to place the registry fee so high that the ordinary member of the Ayrshire

Association cannot reach it. We cannot weed out the worthless animals by raising the recording fee. We must trust to the honesty of the breeder himself to do the weeding. We cannot weed out the worthless animals by a recording fee,—Never! It must be by the efforts of the breeder himself. While it makes but little difference to the wealthy man, yet this Association is made up of men of moderate means, men who have just started in the breeding of Ayrshire cattle. If we raise this recording fee to $5.00, it will frighten away new members and some of our own members of moderate means. It is the wealthy man who makes a monopoly of the bull trade, and this would concentrate that trade with the wealthy men. Let us have all bulls recorded, and when they have made their impress upon the stock we can tell whether they are valuable or not. I have seen Ayrshire calves go into the show ring that promised well, but I have seen those animals fairly used up by the time they were four or five years old. I have seen others who showed but little indication of good, and the form was not right as a calf at three months, or even as yearlings, and I have seen those animals improve until when they reached maturity they were animals that we would be proud to put at the head of our herds; and so I trust this action will not be taken for the good of the Association at large.

Mr. Pember—The report of the Committee makes a recommendation, and I move that the recommendation of the Committee be accepted.

Motion put and carried.

Mr. Pember—I was present at the meeting last year with many of you here this afternoon, when our President made his report, recognizing the difficulty that we are facing, and that is of having distributed through the country a lot of inferior bull calves at an inferior price. When we pick up our papers and find breeders advertising their calves for $15 apiece, it takes the courage out of some of us who are trying to do better. The President made a report suggesting that $5.00 registry fee be asked for members, and of course that would make $10.00 for those who are not members. I had the honor to make a motion that this recommendation be adopted, and it was carried; but I am very sorry that I made that motion. If you will permit me to make a confession,—I am sorry I took the stand I did last year. In facing the facts and looking the thing over more carefully, I am convinced that I made a mistake, and that we shall make a mistake if we adopt the suggestions of our Committee. Of this I am firmly convinced,—that we would not get at the difficulty, that we would not heal the disease at all. If that amount must be paid, we will pay it, and sell the poor bulls just the same. It rests entirely upon the honor of the breeder, and the whole thing turns right there. If a man is not honest enough with himself and the Ayrshire breed to dispose properly of inferior calves, we shall not heal the difficulty by making him pay a little more to get his scrub creature before the public.

Mr. Converse—I believe the man is not born that can tell the real value of a bull at three months, without he has the opportunity of examining both the sire and the dam. You may find an inferior calf at three months that looks unfit for the slaughter house turn out to be one of the best bulls ever raised. I had the pleasure of being in Montreal recently at the new McDowell College, and I believe the man at the head of that college is as good a man as can be produced in America, and the college is well endowed, and Mr. McDowell said to me: "We are not here to make money, and you fellows can't buy any more bull calves of us. We are here to help the farmer, and we are going to sell our bull calves at a price at which they will buy them. We bargain with them to keep the bull two years, and then if they want to go back to scrub breeding, let them go.'' In our own case, we sell our bull calves to a man who begins at the foot of the ladder, so to speak, and they raise up a grand dairy of cows, and from that inspiration grows on them to employ only the best bull they can find. Therefore, Mr. Chairman, I move you as an amendment to the motion, that this matter be laid on the table.

Mr. Pike—I think three years ago at Boston I introduced this same resolution myself. Since then I have had a change of heart, and am not in favor of it at all. I live up in St. Lawrence County, in a town where there are five large herds of registered Ayrshires. When we can sell off our bull calves, we are willing to sell them to our farmer neighbors for what they are worth to them to head their herds, and you will find some greater Ayrshire cows up there than you will find in any other town in the United States. The city of New York sends a representative up to St. Lawrence County, and he says we have the best kept dairy herds in the State of New York and of this country,—and they go to every section of the country.

Mr. Spalding—The bull is worth what the dairy product is worth to the dairy farmer. It is the production of the dairy farm that counts. If you shut the farmer out and charge him a $5.00 fee, he will go to his Jersey friend over there who only charges him $1.00. I think you will do an injustice to the dairy farmer of this country and shut him out of a good supply of good dairy stock.

The President—Mr. Pember moved to accept the recommendation of the Committee. It is moved to lay this motion on the table.

Motion seconded and carried.

THE PRESIDENT—There is a Committee on Tuberculosis. Will the Secretary please read the printed report?

AYRSHIRE BREEDERS' ASSOCIATION

DEAR SIR:—The following resolution was unanimously adopted by the Executive Committee of the Ayrshire Breeders' Association, at its last meeting held in Philadelphia, Pa., on the 26th day of November, 1907, and a copy thereof directed to be sent to each member of the Association, in order that the important matters embodied therein may come up for discussion at the next annual meeting:

"WHEREAS, irreparable loss has been sustained by the dairymen and breeders of dairy cattle, in this, as well as in other countries, through the ravages of bovine tuberculosis, and

WHEREAS, modern science has discovered a method whereby cattle can be examined and the presence of this dread disease detected without in any wise injuring the life or health of the animal tested, and

WHEREAS, by destroying or isolating the animals affected we can prevent the spread of this disease and eventually eradicate it entirely from our Ayrshire herds by the use of proper methods, and

WHEREAS, to eliminate this disease from our herds would strengthen the claim that Ayrshire cattle are freer from disease and more hardy than any other breed of dairy cattle, and would also be the means of keeping disease out of those herds which are now in a healthy condition.

Now Therefore, the Executive Committee of the Ayrshire Breeders' Association recommend to every breeder and owner of Ayrshire cattle the establishment of the following rules:

First: As soon as possible to test every animal in his herd with tuberculin, eliminating therefrom every animal which reacts to the test.

Second: To test his herd at intervals of not exceeding one year, to ascertain any subsequent cases of tuberculosis that may have started in his herd. In the event that there were reactions at the time of the first test, to retest his herd within six months from the date of the first test.

Third: To sell no animal for breeding purposes that has reacted, or with respect to which there is any question as to its complete health.

Fourth: To admit no animal into the herd from other herds, unless the same has been found to be free from tuberculosis upon a test made by a qualified and reputable veterinarian. To purchase no animal except subject to its passing the tuberculin examination and to make a further test of each animal so purchased from four to six months after acquiring the same; it being strongly recommended to isolate animals so purchased until such further test is made and determined before the same are allowed to enter the herd.

Fifth: To keep stable premises and barn yards at all times in a sanitary condition, and to disinfect stable thoroughly not less than once every three months whether tuberculosis has been found or not. Likewise to observe care in pasturing animals in fields where tuberculous or suspicious cattle are being kept; likewise to observe that the water supply for the cattle has not been polluted by tuberculous cattle, especially the supply gotten from watering troughs.

SIXTH: Destruction of all tuberculous cattle is advocated, and the removal and burning of the carcass. If the breeders can not afford to do this would advocate the 'Bang System' vigorously followed.

SEVENTH: Every breeder is requested to report promptly to the Executive Committee or to the President of the Association, any case of fraud on the part of any other breeder in the sale of tuberculous cattle to him, in order that such member may be removed from the Association and his misfeasance brought to the attention of other breeders.

EIGHTH: If in doubt as to how to proceed, each breeder is invited to communicate immediately with your President, or Secretary, who will be glad to advise him on this important matter.

NINTH: Every breeder should advise the Secretary of the Association upon receiving this communication as to his views on this matter, or better still, come to the next annual meeting and present them in person.

The above resolution was drafted by Mr. L. A. Reymann, of Wheeling, West Virginia, in accordance with the vote of the Executive Committee, which resolution was to be printed in circular form and mailed to each member of the Association.

C. M. WINSLOW,
Secretary.

Brandon, Vt., December 16, 1907.

Mr. Reymann—Only two responded to me, I think, from the communications sent out by the Secretary. It is introduced in the same spirit as the other proposition was,—in a spirit of discussion. I would like to say on the last proposition, just so that we are not misunderstood: What we wanted was to get at some method by which we can alleviate or better a condition which is existing. What we wanted to do was to get a discussion with respect to that. Now the recommendation of the Committee was merely a suggestion, and I am pleased to see there is so much spirit in respect to it. What the Committee wants is to get a full discussion from all points of view and to get at the facts.

Mr. Valentine—I move that the report be adopted and filed.

Motion seconded and carried.

The President—I wish to say that as President, I will appoint a Committee of three,—this was a resolution of the Executive Committee in Philadelphia, to appoint three members who shall have charge of appointing at least five or more judges for fairs, to be published in the Year Book. I name Mr. Howard Cook, Dr. Jerome F. Butterfield and Mr. Geo. H. Converse.

Mr. Converse—It seems fitting at this time that we should have a Committee appointed to prepare suitable memorials for those of our members who have passed away since the last meeting, and that special mention should be made of those who were charter members. I move that the Chair appoint such a Committee.

Motion seconded and carried.

The President—I will appoint Mr. Converse, of New York; Mr. Pember, of Maine, and Mr. Valentine, of Pennsylvania, as this Committee of three.

Mr. Pember—I will accept a place on that Committee if we are not to report at this session. I do not wish to act hastily.

The President—You are to file with the Secretary the result of your deliberations.

The President—The question of amending the constitution as to proxies was offered in the form of a resolution at the last annual meeting. The Secretary will read the form of notice given.

The Secretary—The motion to amend the constitution in relation to proxies was to strike out representation by proxy in each article of the constitution.

The President—It is purely a question of proxies.

Mr. Pike—I move that the motion suggested be laid on the table forever.

Motion seconded and carried.

The Secretary—Mr. Valentine has called my attention to the point that at the last meeting we voted that a cow to be eligible to Advanced Registry should have a calf within 15 months from the beginning of test. That was not constitutional and we did not consider it in the Dairy Test.

The President—The election of officers now comes before the meeting.

Dr. Turnbull—It is getting late and we have several articles to hear, and I would like to propose and nominate the following for the several offices: E. J. Fletcher, for President; for Vice-Presidents, Geo. E. Pike, Geo. H. McFadden, E. F. Pember and J. F. Converse; for Secretary, C. M. Winslow; Treasurer, Nicholas S. Winsor; Auditor, George H. Yeaton; balance of Executive Committee, John R. Valentine, L. A. Reymann, Howard Cook,

W. P. Schanck, J. F. Butterfield and Charles H. Hayes; and move that the Secretary be directed to cast the vote of the Association for these officers.

Mr. Oakey—I move that we proceed to the election of officers, one at a time, and I would nominate for President of this Association a man whom I think is well qualified, and a man who this year has shown a great deal of public spirit in the interests of the Association, Mr. L. A. Reymann, of Wheeling, West Virginia.

The President—Any other nominations for President?

Mr. Valentine—Have those nominations been seconded?

Mr. Wells—I would like to second the nomination of Mr. Reymann. He was instrumental this year in giving the best Ayrshire exhibit ever held at Chicago.

Mr. Pike—Mr. Reymann is a jolly good fellow, and I almost want to vote for him myself; but I want to nominate Mr. Fletcher, who is interested in the Ayrshire Association, and has been for many years; he is a young man, and would make an excellent President.

Mr. Wells—I move that we take an informal ballot for President, and that the President appoint two tellers.

The President—I will appoint Mr. Howard Cook, of Ohio, and Mr. Wells, of Connecticut, and proceed to an informal ballot.

The question is whether the proxies will be used in this election. We never have used proxies in that sense in the past, as I understand it.

Mr. ———: Mr. President, this is not an election. This is an informal ballot, and then we have to proceed to election afterwards.

Mr. Pember—Do you mean to rule out the proxies?

The President—I asked for the sense of the meeting.

Mr. Valentine—I want to say that I feel for one,—and I think I can say that the Committee who sent out the notices for proxies feel that we have been placed in a rather false position. At the meeting of the Executive Committee at the Bingham House, in Philadelphia, all of the members present apparently acquiesced in a resolution proposed by Mr. McFadden that a Committee from the Executive Committee be appointed to solicit proxies. These proxies were to be voted, if they were voted at all according to the instructions of the maker of the proxy; in the absence of that, to be voted by this Committee. When these proxies were sent out the Committee did not know that the Secretary had sent out a notice soliciting proxies in his own behalf. That made it look as though there was some friction between the Executive Committee and the Secretary. I was entirely ignorant of any such condition when I accepted a position on this Committee, and I think that Mr. Reymann and Mr. Wells felt the same way about it, at the time. I did not know but what Mr. Winslow would send it out in his call. Mr. Ballou, Mr. Wells and Mr. Reymann wrote me to prepare to send it out. I did not know that individuals were soliciting proxies, and I think it puts this Committee in a very awkward position for the Secretary to have solicited proxies, and to have acquiesced in that motion at that time.

Mr. Pike—It has been the custom of this Association for the Secretary in sending out his notices of the annual meeting and notification to enclose a proxy without any instructions whatever, giving each member the privilege he enjoys of using that proxy if he so chooses. To my knowledge, Mr. Winslow has never solicited anybody's proxy for the purpose of using it for himself, or for any other purpose, and I do not think he did so this year. If he has done so it has not come to my notice. I am here to represent the five Gouverneur breeders, and a good many others whose proxies I have and who are opposed to such radical action as was expressed, or rather implied, in the notices sent out by the Executive Committee. The gentleman says that the action of the Executive Committee was unanimous, but failed to say that all the members did not attend the meeting in Philadelphia, and the notice that was sent to all the members neglected to say that not all the members were present at the meeting. It carried the impression that it was the unanimous action of the Executive Committee of this Association. We have all discovered that the members are very much opposed to being deprived of that representation, and they never will allow it, and if any such thing should be allowed in this Association it would disrupt it instantly. I do not think there has been any feeling excepting that engendered by the call and the second call from the Executive Committee soliciting proxies to vote us all out of representation.

Mr. VALENTINE—The proxies were not solicited for that purpose.

Mr. PIKE—It had that appearance.

Mr. VALENTINE—In the second call it stated that they would be pleased to vote them in accordance with the instructions of the member.

Mr. CONVERSE—I move that the vote be taken to-day just as we have elected officers for the last thirty-three years.

Mr. PIKE—While that motion might be carried, we could not justify the action. As I said, I am here representing five Gouverneur breeders, and you cannot pass a resolution depriving me of voting those proxies.

Mr. Wells—Possibly the proxies have not been used, but their use has been authorized, and it is not pleasant for fifteen or twenty of us to go away and say that the votes were buttoned up in our overcoat pockets.

Mr. Converse—We have always trusted our officials and we can trust them still. They have never used the proxies, and I think we can trust them. I understand at Philadelphia last year there were only 25 members present—just above a quorum under favorable circumstances. In some circumstances the proxies might come into use, but I do not favor using the proxies in the election of our officers because then it throws the matter into the hands of a few men. There has never been any discord and I hope there will be no hurt feelings among the members. I am a Quaker in spirit, if not in creed, and I am under the impression that our officers to-day, or our officers in the future whom we may elect, will never make improper use of proxies in electing officers for this Society or in adopting methods that will not be for the good of this Association. I believe in proxies, we have always had them. We have members scattered over 31 states, in the United States and Canada. It is impossible for some of these men ever to attend our meetings, and I do not believe in depriving these men of representation in this Ayrshire Association. I voted for the proxies, and I voted for them with the confidence that our officers would never make improper use of them, and I do not believe that they will; but I think we should have them simply as a precaution, in case of a block on the railway, or a snow storm, or a strike, that might keep a quorum of members away.

Mr. Pember—I am anxious to do just what is right in this matter, not only by myself but by others, and there is a breeder in Maine who could not come 500 miles to this meeting, who sent me a letter with a special request that I should represent him, and in the election of officers or other important business should vote for him. He also enclosed a formal proxy and I hold that proxy. Now is that all that that means? Can I go back home and say that is all it means? There has been no strike on the railroad, there has been no snow storm, but I must say "I could not vote for you." It is certain that proxies mean something or nothing. Shall I vote it or not? That is the point. If I am honest by my brother I cast my own vote and the vote of Mr. Buckley whose proxy I hold.

THE PRESIDENT—There is a question before the house, that a formal ballot be taken for President. The Tellers will please collect the votes.

MR. WELLS—I find that we are proceeding in the wrong way.

MR. PEMBER—May I have the attention of the members just a second. I want to know whether I am going to vote the proxy placed in my hands or not. I do not want to do a dishonest thing or a thing that is not done anywhere and by every right. I came here expecting to vote for Mr. Buckley. I consider that the election of President is an important matter and unless it be decided to the contrary, I shall vote my proxy.

MR. VALENTINE—What has been the custom in the past?

MR. ———: I think if we had used our proxies before, we would have no discussion now.

MR. YEATON—Much stress has been placed upon that motion of the Executive Committee in Philadelphia. It was a unanimous vote. There must have been a necessity to ask for proxies. I do not see why we should not go ahead and use them and see where we stand.

Mr. Dorrance—The constitution of this Association gives me the right to send my vote here by proxy, provided I cannot come, and one of my neighbors who could not come appointed me to vote in his place and asked me to do so, and I do not know any reason why I should not.

The President—There is no question about the right of an absent member to send his proxy here. It is only a question of custom. If you want to go into proxies——

Mr. Valentine—Why not proceed to ballot?

The President—If you take an informal ballot, and it is close, then you can go further.

Mr. Burke—I move the members vote at the table instead of passing the hat around.

Mr. Pember—I voted in favor of taking a formal ballot, and I move to rescind that vote. Let us get on square ground.

The President—It is moved and seconded that we take an informal ballot.

Motion carried.

Members proceed to cast their ballots.

The President—The polls are closed. The tellers will count the votes.

The President—The report of the tellers:

Whole number of votes cast 36, informal vote for

MR. FLETCHER, 22.

MR. REYMANN, 14.

Mr. Reymann—I move that the vote for Mr. Fletcher be made unanimous and that the Secretary be instructed to cast the unanimous ballot of the Association for Mr. Fletcher for President of the Association.

Motion seconded and carried.

THE PRESIDENT—The Chair will now appoint Mr. Cook, of Ohio, and Mr. Pember, of Maine, to escort Mr. Fletcher to the chair.

MR. PEMBER—Maine has the pleasure of presenting New Hampshire with the Presidency.

MR. FLETCHER—Gentlemen, I thank you for the honor, and I shall try to be worthy and work for the advancement of the Ayrshires.

You will please prepare and bring in your ballots for First Vice-President.

MR. BELL—If there is no objection, I move that the Secretary cast one ballot for George E. Pike for First Vice-President.

Motion put and carried.

DR. TURNBULL—I would like to nominate for remaining Vice-Presidents, Mr. E. F. Pember, Mr. George H. McFadden and Mr. J. F. Converse.

MR. SPALDING—I should like to nominate Dr. Turnbull for the remaining Vice-President.

Motion seconded and carried.

MR. BELL—This cannot be done unless we have a unanimous vote.

MR. ———: I nominate Mr. Pember for Second Vice-President.

MR. OAKEY—I nominate George W. Ballou.

THE PRESIDENT—Please prepare and bring in your ballots for Second Vice-President.

MR. BALLOU—I decline the position, Mr. Chairman.

MR. OAKEY—I move the nominations be closed and the Secretary be instructed to cast one ballot for Dr. Turnbull for Second Vice-President.

Dr. Turnbull—I move to nominate for Third Vice-President George H. McFadden.

Mr. Dorrance—For Fourth Vice-President, I would like to nominate one of our Charter Members, the oldest member in the Empire State, Mr. J. F. Converse.

The President—It has been moved and seconded that the Secretary cast one vote for Mr. Converse for Fourth Vice-President.

The Secretary cast vote as directed.

The President—Gentlemen, please prepare and bring in your ballots for Secretary.

Mr. Yeaton—I move that the President cast one ballot for Mr. C. M. Winslow, as your Secretary.

Motion put and carried.

Vote cast by President as directed.

The Secretary—Gentlemen, I thank you for this, and I am Secretary to every member in this Association. I want to be as much the Secretary to one member as I am to another, and any time when you find a man you prefer, I wish you would tell me. I do not want to hold the office to the injury of the Association. I have worked hard for the Association always, and I have done as well as I could, and I will be very glad if anybody will give me any points or touch me up if I do anything that is not for the interests of the Association.

The President—Please prepare and bring in your ballots for Treasurer.

Dr. Turnbull—I nominate Mr. N. S. Winsor, and move that the Secretary be instructed to cast one vote for Mr. Winsor for Treasurer.

Motion seconded and carried.

Secretary cast ballot.

THE PRESIDENT—Please prepare and bring in your ballots for Auditor.

DR. TURNBULL—I would like to nominate Mr. George H. Yeaton, and move that the Secretary cast one vote for Mr. Yeaton as Auditor.

Motion seconded and carried.

Secretary cast vote.

THE PRESIDENT—Please prepare and bring in your ballots for members of the Executive Committee for three years. Those to go out this year are Charles H. Hayes and Everett B. Sherman.

MR. REYMANN—I should like to nominate Mr. John W. Oakey, and Mr. Charles H. Hayes to succeed himself.

MR. YEATON—I would like to nominate Dr. J. F. Butterfield for the second man.

Moved and seconded that the Secretary cast one vote for Mr. Charles H. Hayes as member of the Executive Committee.

Carried.

THE PRESIDENT—Please prepare and bring in your ballots for member of the Executive Committee for three years.

DR. BUTTERFIELD—I withdraw my name.

MR. REYMANN—Then I move the Secretary cast one vote for John W. Oakey for member of the Executive Committee for three years.

Motion seconded and carried.

Secretary cast vote.

THE PRESIDENT—That completes the election of officers.

Mr. VALENTINE—Mr. President, Mr. Winslow has asked me if I would bring up the question of the Home Dairy Test. He says it has been the custom every year to decide whether we shall go on, and so in order to get the matter on a permanent basis I will make a motion that the Home Dairy Test be established as the basis for all tests of the Ayrshire Breeders' Association for the future.

Seconded and carried.

MR. YEATON—I would like to inquire if it is customary to appoint the Home Dairy Test Committee at this meeting? It seems to me that three at the most would be just as well. I move that Mr. Winslow and Dr. Turnbull constitute the Home Dairy Test Committee for the ensuing year.

MR. REYMANN—What has been the custom up to now?

THE PRESIDENT—There have been three members.

MR. REYMANN—I do not think we had better release any of the safeguards that have been thrown about these tests. It is true it may be a little additional expense, but it is expense put in the proper place and well expended. There is no reason why this Committee should be reduced, and unless there is some particular reason outside of the expense that goes with it I do not think it should be done. I would like to see every breeder test his cattle, and a man might be put on this Committee who has not engaged in these tests. One of the men proposed is a particular friend of mine whose honor and integrity I value highly. But he is a member of the Committee.

THE SECRETARY—One of the rules of the Home Dairy Test is that a member of the Committee shall not personally supervise his own tests.

Mr. Reymann—There is the proposition I was getting at. Mr. Winslow being on the Committee, it would hardly seem right to have a member on the Committee passing on his own tests. We want to encourage these tests, we want every man who enters his cattle to feel that he is getting a good chance to win. We do not want him to have any suspicions. He may not know Mr. Winslow as well as I know him. I have my herd tested. I have a number of animals put in the Advanced Registry with pretty good records. I know these records are correct; but for the man who does not know these things, we want to convince him that the Committee is so large that it is not one particular member passing on these propositions,—the larger the Committee the more confidence there would be on the part of those who have not engaged in the tests heretofore with respect to the test itself, and therefore I would suggest that the original number of the Committee be retained.

Mr. Yeaton—I accept the amendment, and suggest that Mr. Reymann be the third man.

The Secretary—I would like to second Mr. Reymann's nomination for the Home Dairy Test Committee. He has shown great interest in it, and that is the kind of men we want on the Committee,—men who are interested in it and who are pushing their cattle. Mr. Reymann has done a lot of work, he has entered his cows, he holds the championship for the two-year-old record, and I think a man who takes such an interest in testing cattle is just the man to be on that Committee.

Mr. Reymann—In order to be consistent, I will be compelled to decline.

The President—The question before the house is that the Committee consist of Dr. Turnbull, Mr. Winslow and Mr. Reymann.

Mr. Wells—I move that Mr. Reymann be relieved from the Committee if he does not wish to serve.

Mr. Reymann—I would request that somebody else be put on that Committee. I am in earnest about this, though I appreciate the kindly sentiment here. I have business at home, and I must say that my trip here has been a personal sacrifice; but I wanted to be present, and I would like to have my name withdrawn, because if I am on a proposition of that kind I do not want to be put in a position of lagging behind, and I know that there are breeders more conveniently situated to more readily confer with either representative; so if I may be permitted to withdraw in favor of some other man,——

The Secretary—It is a matter of a good deal of importance that the men who are on that Committee be men whose heart and soul is in the progress of the Ayrshire cow.

Mr. Dorrance—I think it is very unfortunate if Mr. Reymann declines, but I do not think it is showing courtesy to him, if he asks us to release him——

Mr. Pike—I move the nomination of Mr. Valentine in place of Mr. Reymann.

Mr. Valentine—I must decline the nomination. I am sincere. I am not in a position where it would be possible to give it any attention this coming year.

The Secretary—I nominate Mr. Probasco.

Motion seconded and carried, electing Mr. Probasco as the third member of the Home Dairy Test Committee.

Mr. Pike—I want to make a suggestion with regard to the appointment by the President of three gentlemen as Judges. I think it would be well enough for this Committee to be in a position to recommend Judges in each state. For instance, I know a man who is showing Shorthorn cattle. He goes down in the southern states and he shows those cattle as Shorthorns, or Ayrshires, or Jerseys, as is most convenient, and I know where his son sold one of those abominable things,—sold it in the state of Pennsylvania for an Ayrshire! and got a good round price for it. The man who bought that animal will despise the Ayrshires the rest of his life. We want Judges who are available in the different states.

THE SECRETARY—The motion was that the President appoint a Committee of three who should name a Committee of five or more to report at the Annual Meeting. It is proper for the Committee to report the five men here.

MR. BALLOU—I was not to report here the three names before the Annual Meeting. It was intended that the Committee prepare at their leisure a Committee of experts who would be available for the Year Book.

THE SECRETARY—Whenever the time was, it was to be reported to the Association for their ratification.

MR. BALLOU—The selection of Judges is a serious matter, and you cannot do it in a day. You may need an expert to find out who are the best people to send in to the Secretary for publication in the Year Book.

THE SECRETARY—They were to have been reported for the meeting to concur in the nomination.

MR. BALLOU—I was not to report before this meeting.

THE SECRETARY—Mr. Ballou was asked to name a Committee of three who should select a Committee of five to report at the next Annual Meeting, for their concurrence. Mr. Ballou said he would like time to select that Committee.

Mr. DORRANCE—It seems impossible to have that Committee nominated at this time, and I move that the Committee be given time to prepare that list to be placed in the Year Book, but I cannot see that the meeting can ratify it.

Mr. REYMANN—I suggest that that Committee report to the Executive Committee, and let them approve.

Mr. DORRANCE—I accept the amendment.

Motion seconded and carried.

Dr. TURNBULL—Before we finish up the business,—we have two or three gentlemen with us this afternoon—we have taken up a great deal of their time—I move that we now hear Dr. Dexter, who represents in the Department of Agriculture the Dairy Division, and that we listen to what he has to tell us about the uniform tests.

THE PRESIDENT—Mr. Winslow would like to know how many are going to remain for the banquet to-night.

Mr. REYMANN—At what time is it to be, Mr. Winslow?

THE PRESIDENT—At six o'clock.

THE SECRETARY—But we cannot get through here at six o'clock.

THE PRESIDENT—All those who intend to stay to the banquet, please raise their hands.

THE SECRETARY—These cups ought to be presented, and I would suggest that Mr. Ballou, being on the Home Dairy Test Committee and President of the Association, present this cup to Mr. Oakey for Mr. McFadden.

Mr. BALLOU—This donation, as I understand it, is contributed by all the members of this Association through the Home Dairy Test Committee. It has been fairly won by Mr. George H. McFadden, of Philadelphia, and we are delighted that it should go to such a beautiful place as the Barclay Farm, for we were all there last year, and the only thing we failed to find was a cup like that. We wish it was even a little bigger, and that it could be filled at times. But Mr. McFadden was so generous and kindly in giving us entertainment, and showing us his cattle, I think everybody here is glad to see this cup go to so worthy a member. The cup goes to Mr. Oakey who is here in behalf of Mr. McFadden.

This French cup came from the French Fund of which you all know, I suppose. It is a permanent fund. These cups are to be handed around in the future,—to those who win them, of course. Mr. Fletcher, your President, wins this one. He gets his crown as he comes into office, —I did not get any. But he won it fairly,—I remember being on the Committee when it was figured out. I had never seen Mr. Fletcher, but he did such a fine piece of work in the test, that he is deserving of it. Gentlemen, Mr. Fletcher has won his cup and I am glad to present him with it.

THE SECRETARY—Mr. Valentine has a family of cows named "Ivan," and Mr. Karr has another family of "Ivans." The cows are not related, and Mr. Valentine would like to have the Association authorize a change in the name of his family to "Ithan." I see no objection, and I move that the Secretary be authorized to change the name of Mr. Valentine's Ivan family to Ithan.

Motion seconded and carried.

MR. YEATON—I have heard quite a number of members speak of the Advanced Registry cows,—that they have not been put in the Herd Book, and I find there is quite a feeling that all who are entitled to Advanced Registry should appear in each Volume as they come in. Last year we tried to keep the Herd Book down small enough to get them in, but it ran away from us. I would suggest that the Advanced Registry cows come out temporarily in the Year Book, and when we get enough for a volume that we report it in a volume. The members do not use the Herd Book very much, but if they are put into the Year Book they will be brought before every man in the country, and I would suggest that the Secretary be authorized to publish Advanced Registry cows in the Year Book.

MR. DORRANCE—If these Advanced Registry cow records were printed every year, it would not take more than half a dozen leaves, would it? It would not add but little to the bulk of the volume.

THE SECRETARY—It was thought best to have photographs of cows that had qualified, and we have been trying to get them but have not been successful. That is one reason why they have been kept back. Another is that Vol. XVIII filled so fast after notice of closing that the addition of the Advanced Registry entries would make the volume larger than the Association voted to keep it.

MR. DORRANCE—It would seem to be a good idea to keep these Advanced Registry records and put the photographs in the Year Book. If there is a sufficient number to make it advisable to publish these in every volume of the Ayrshire record, I think it ought to be put in every record, as I think the Advanced Registry is one of the most important things the Ayrshire Breeders are doing, and I would move that the Volume XIX be closed and that room be saved for the Advanced Registry animals in Volume XIX.

THE PRESIDENT—All those in favor of closing Volume XIX and leaving space enough to add any Advanced Registry cows, please manifest it by saying "Aye."

Voted and carried.

Mr. Converse—Have we had any notice of the closing of the Herd Book? Mr. Secretary, may I ask if you have published any notice that you proposed to close the Herd Book?

The Secretary—The motion was that the Secretary be authorized to close the Herd Book, in order that he could keep a certain number of pages. The Association voted some years ago authorizing the Secretary to close each volume when it reached about 425 to 450 pages, in order to keep the volumes uniform and to prevent them from being cumbersome in size.

Motion carried.

Mr. Pember—I will detain you but a moment. I wish to present for membership in our Association the name of Mr. Joseph G. Ray, of Portland, Maine.

Motion seconded and carried to accept Mr. Ray as a member.

The President—I am requested to say that our Treasurer has several copies of Vol. XVIII Ayrshire Records that he would like to dispose of, if any one would like them.

Mr. Yeaton—I move that as Mr. Dexter is ready to talk, we give him the floor.

Mr. Dexter—I am in doubt as to whether I should take the floor. I gather from what was said a moment ago that the hotel is waiting to come in here to set the tables in this room, and the matter on which I have come by the invitation of the Secretary affects not only the Ayrshire Breeders' Association, but all the other Associations of breeders of dairy cattle; and I should be very sorry to detain the members of this Association by asking them to listen to me now, if there be an opportunity at or after the banquet. I will be perfectly willing to discuss it around the banquet table, if you will so adjourn that they can do the business then.

Mr. Converse—I move that we hear this paper at the table, for we are keeping these people waiting.

Motion put and carried.

Dr. Turnbull—I move that we take a rest to meet at the banquet table.

Motion put and carried.

The President—I declare a "rest" until time for the banquet.

The Special Prizes at Chicago were awarded as follows:

R. R. NESS.

1st on herd of four cows in milk	$50 00
1st on breeders' young herd	40 00
1st on calf herd owned and bred by exhibitor	20 00
1st champion bull, over 3 years	25 00
1st champion bull, under 2 years	25 00
	$160 00

W. P. SCHANCK.

2nd on herd of four cows in milk	$30 00
2nd on breeders' young herd	30 00
3rd on calf herd owned and bred by exhibitor	10 00
1st on best 3 heifers in milk, get of one sire	40 00
1st champion female, over 3 years	25 00
1st champion female, under 3 years	25 00
	$160 00

R. HUNTER & SONS.

3rd on four cows in milk	$20 00
3rd on breeder's young herd	20 00
2nd on best 3 heifers in milk, get one sire	30 00
	$70 00

GEO. H. McFADDEN.

4th on breeders' young herd	$10 00
2nd on calf herd owned and bred by exhibitor	15 00
3rd on best 3 heifers in milk, get of one sire	20 00
	$45 00

HILLVIEW STOCK FARM (Ltd.)

4th on calf herd owned and bred by exhibitor	$5 00

R. H. MASON OF MISSOURI UNIVERSITY

Won the special prize for best

Student Judge of dairy cattle	$50 00
Hillview Stock Farm (Ltd.)	5 00
Geo. H. McFadden	45 00
R. Hunter & Sons	70 00
W. P. Schanck	160 00
R. R. Ness	160 00
	$490 00

JOHN W. OAKEY,
WM. T. WELLS,
GEO. WM. BALLOU,
                  Committee.

Paper read by Dr. Dexter, of Washington, D. C.

NATIONAL DAIRY REGISTER OF MERIT.

In order to promote uniformity as to the standards of dairy excellence and methods of testing dairy cows, and to provide for national registration of official records, the National Dairy Register of Merit is established by the United States Department of Agriculture in co-operation with the associations of breeders of dairy cattle in the United States.

The National Dairy Register of Merit shall be based on yearly records only. The year for test shall consist of 365 days without restriction as to periods of lactation or the calving of the cows. Tests shall be supervised by men connected as representatives with State Agricultural Colleges or Experiment Stations, and their reports shall be countersigned by the director of such institution or the head of its dairy department. Neither this official supervisor nor the institution he represents shall have any financial interest in the cattle tested.

Tests for the proposed register shall be made only of full-blooded cattle registered in associations co-operating in this national dairy register of merit. Each application for such test shall go through the hands of such a breeders' association. The breeders' association in each case shall make application to the official in charge of such tests in the state from which the application comes, and report such application to the United States Department of Agriculture. The breeders' association shall be responsible to the experiment station or agricultural college supervising the test for the payment of the costs of the test.*

---

*Arrangements as to expenses of each test and limit of number of cows to be tested at any one time shall be left to the supervising institution in conference with the association to which cows being tested belong.

The length of time for actual expert supervision shall be two days for each month in the year of test. The milk record of the owner of the cattle shall be accepted as the record for the year, provided it agrees practically with that taken by the official expert supervisor for the two days each month. The butter fat record for the year shall be determined by multiplying the milk record for each month by the average percentage of butter fat shown in the tests of the milkings for the two days supervised by the official expert. No second test or inspection shall be allowed in any month.

Cows may be admitted to the register on the production of a minimum amount of either butter fat or milk; but all the essential facts of the performance, including the production of solids not fat and the complete feeding and breeding record shall be reported.

The minimum standard for mature cows five years old or over, shall be 360 lbs. butter fat or 10,000 lbs. milk. The minimum standard for cows two years old or under shall be 250 lbs. butter fat or 6,500 lbs. milk.

For each day the cow tested is over two years old at the beginning of her year's record the amount of milk she will be required to produce in this year will be established by adding 3.2 lbs. for every such day to the 6,500 lbs. required when two years old.

This ration is applicable until the animal is five years old, when the required amount will have reached 10,000 lbs.

For each day the cow tested is over two years old at the beginning of the year's record, the amount of butter fat she will be required to produce in the year will be established by adding .1 of 1 lb. for each such day to the 250 lbs. required when two years old. This ratio is applicable until the amount required reaches 360 lbs. butter fat at the age of 5 years.

For the purpose of estimating the amount of butter produced the rule provided by the association of agricultural colleges and experiment stations may be followed, viz.: "Add one-sixth of the amount of butter fat." It should be understood, however, that in all records made for or published in the National Dairy Register of Merit the amount of butter fat produced and not the estimate of butter be given.

A full record of the test shall be made each month on uniform blanks acceptable to all the breeders' associations co-operating, and mailed to the officer in charge of such work at the supervising institution; and carbon copies of the same shall be furnished by such officer to the owner of the tested cow, to the secretary of the breeders' association to which the tested cow belongs, and to the United States Department of Agriculture, at the close of each month; and if such record be not so mailed it shall be at the discretion of the breeders' association or the United States Department of Agriculture to discontinue the test.

Any registry may be delayed for investigation at the request of the secretary of the breeders' association directly interested, or of the Secretary of the United States Department of Agriculture; and any incorrect entry may be expunged from the proposed register and the certificate of such entry revoked, by the direction of the Secretary of the United States Department of Agriculture, upon evidence of its incorrectness.

Questions not covered by the rules agreed upon in conference shall be determined by the Secretary of the United States Department of Agriculture, in consultation with the secretary of the association represented in the test.

When the year's test is completed the United States Department of Agriculture will furnish a certificate of merit to the owner of the cow tested, through the breeders' association, setting forth the details of the record of the test, including a description of the cow, her breed, age, register number, and such other facts as the Secretary of the United States Department of Agriculture may deem necessary to prevent fraud in the use of the certificate. A photograph of the cow shall be furnished by the owner to be affixed to the certificate.

RESOLVED: That it is the judgment of this Association that the Dairy Division of the Bureau of Animal Industry of the United States Department of Agriculture should be raised to the full rank of a Bureau; and the Secretary of the United States Department of Agriculture is hereby respectfully requested to recommend such action by the Congress of the United States as will accomplish this change.

A vote of thanks was given Dr. Dexter for his interesting and instructive talk.

RESOLVED: That this Association respectfully requests the Secretary of the United States Department of Agriculture to co-operate in the work of the National Dairy Register of Merit, as proposed in the action just taken; and that he provide for the necessary correspondence and office work involved in conducting the proposed National Dairy Register of Merit, and to publish this register from time to time in bulletins or otherwise as may be required.

ADDRESS BY W. F. STEPHEN.

At Banquet of American Ayrshire Association.

GENTLEMEN:—

It affords me pleasure to again be with you in annual session to listen to your discussions and take part in your deliberations for the advancement of the breed of dairy cattle in which we have one common interest. I bring you greetings from the Ayrshire breeders of Canada. Although there is a great (tariff) wall between us, yet in kindly greetings and amicable feelings there is no barrier, and I am pleased to say that in these matters we can reciprocate, yea, even international relations and trade in Ayrshires are such that it is now quite practicable for the American and Canadian Ayrshire breeders to do business with each other.

Since we met last year in annual session in the city of "Brotherly Love," the Ayrshire breed has continued to increase in popularity. It would appear that many sections of our continent have just discovered that we have a grand dairy breed in the Ayrshire, full of vitality, constitutional vigor and prepotency, having great powers of digesting and assimilating food and turning it into milk at a good profit over cost of feed, proving they are a most economical breed for the dairy farmer.

Also we have just discovered they are the best breed for the dairyman producing milk for city consumption, as they give a milk full of vitality, also a well-balanced milk, the proportion of butter fat to total solids being well equalized, therefore an easily digested and healthful milk.

To my mind there are three factors that have contributed to popularize the Ayrshire breed; the show ring, the press, and the milk and butter fat records. The show ring,—the Ayrshire breeders of the past have been too modest and they have been exhibitors only in limited numbers in comparison with other dairy breeds. Of late her owner has exhibited her more widely, her attractive appearance, coupled with her kindly disposition and apparent productiveness has attracted attention as never before. Possibly no exhibition ever held on this continent was equal to the display made at the National

Dairy Show at Chicago last October. The Ayrshire exhibit was the admiration of every onlooker and every lover of the dairy cow. All honor to those breeders who contributed to this magnificent showing. And let me say here, that our Ayrshire exhibitors from Canada, who won many of the prizes, were loud in their praises for the kindness and courtesy shown them by the Exhibition Management, and the American exhibitors. Competitors they were for top places, but rivals that exulted in the success of their fellow exhibitor when he reached top place. This is the kind of rivalry that brings out the best that is in a man and is the true spirit of competition.

The Press,—The agricultural press all over our land has given the Ayrshire greater prominence than ever before, by publishing records of her production, calling attention to her merits as a dairy cow, and we quite agree with one writer in the New York Tribune, who stated in his write up of the Ayrshire exhibit at the New York State Fair in 1906: "The exhibit was, in the judgment of the writer, the most significant in the dairy classes. It represented a class of dairy stock that has a place on our dairy farms, a demand not filled by either Jerseys or Holsteins. Animals not capable of phenomenal production, they give neither rich milk nor poor milk; but they will give milk rich enough in solids for sale milk, and from which good returns can be secured when manufactured into butter or cheese. I am not interested in the breed, and do not own an Ayrshire, but it is safe to say that the dairy interests would have profited if as much money had been spent upon Ayrshires as upon either Jerseys or Holsteins." Also the favorable comments on the splendid showing of Ayrshires at the National Dairy Show last fall by all the leading farm papers of the continent, will do much to further the Ayrshire breed. Here again our Ayrshire breeders have been very modest, in fact reticent, in proclaiming through the press the merits of their "favorite breed."

MILK AND BUTTER RECORDS—We Ayrshire breeders have been laggards in this form of proving to the public the possibilities of our breed. I think most of you will agree with me that this is the most important step we have taken, that of establishing a system of recording the production of our cows and heifers. You as an association took the lead among the Ayrshire associations of the world, we soon saw that we must follow in this important work and now the Ayrshire Association of Great Britian and Ireland have adopted a similar system of official testing. Although a comparatively small number of animals have been tested as yet, it has proved to us that we have some phenomenal producers, and a vast host of cows, which with liberal feeding, and kindly attention will be exceedingly profitable animals in the production of milk and butter fat. With milk records adopted by the leading Ayrshire Breeders' Associations—Great Britian and Ireland, Sweden, the American and also the Canadian—we look forward to the Ayrshire owner proving to the public he has a noble dairy breed.

Our Holstein fellow breeders (we wish them all success, as they have a grand breed for milk production), over in Canada lately issued a pamphlet, which was widely circulated, in which they state, "The extent to which a breed spreads through the world and the ease with which it adapts itself to the varying conditions of soil and climate are fairly good tests of its intrinsic worth, particularly is this true with dairy breeds which are found only in civilized countries and on valuable lands. It has been said that the Holstein is found in more countries, occupying more territory, and probably producing more milk, more butter and cheese, than all the other dairy breeds combined." Whether this be true of the Holstein cow or not I am not prepared to say. I would be surprised if it were not so when we consider the Holstein breed dates as far back as the Christian era. But when we again consider that the Ayrshire breed, scarcely one hundred years old, is to be found also in every civilized country in the world, and gaining in popularity as its merits as a dairy breed become known, we are led to realize what a wonderful breed we have.

In conclusion let me say, we must not rest with what has already been accomplished but press on to greater attainments. As we continue to make satisfactory milk and butter records this will denote more and more the true value of our herds.

The Ayrshire Association in Sweden has gone one step in advance of us, as they lately adopted a rule, allowing no animal to be recorded in the Swedish herd book unless it shows the milk record of the dam, paternal and maternal grand dams. I have come to the conclusion in connection with our dairy breeds, the mere recording of pedigree in a herd book is not enough, the best part of the pedigree is the milk record, and butter fat test, and I firmly believe the Ayrshire pedigree of the future will include a milk record. This is not yet but it is coming. We hope to discuss this phase of our pedigrees and possibly take some action in this direction at the annual meeting of the Canadian Ayrshire Breeders' Association to be held in Toronto on February 12th, and we hope to have with us on that occasion representatives from this association. Let our watchword for 1908 be "Advance!" and if spared to meet in session in 1909 we will note with interest the progress of this year."

A banquet of thirty-eight covers was served at which remarks were made by Mr. W. F. Stephen, Secretary of the Canadian Ayrshire Breeders' Association, and Mr. L. A. Reymann, Superintendent of the Ayrshire Exhibit at the Dairy Show at Chicago.

Prof. Wm. H. Dexter, from the United States Department of Agriculture, presented the rules and regulations adopted by the National Dairy Register of Merit, established by the United States Department of Agriculture in co-operation with the association of breeders of dairy cattle in the United States, which were indorsed by the Ayrshire Breeders' Association, and a vote taken to co-operate, in testing cows of this breed, as soon as arrangements can be made.

In the evening the club was entertained by a very interesting and instructive stereopticon lecture by Mr. Valancy Fuller.

The Practical Dairyman, by Mr. Valancy E. Fuller, offered the Ayrshire Breeders' Association space in their paper free of charge for articles and Ayrshire news, and proposed that the Association adopt the Practical Dairyman as their Eastern paper.

The Association accepted their generous offer with thanks, and promised to supply them with articles of interest relating to Ayrshires, but it was not understood that the Association should furnish news to the Practical Dairyman to the exclusion of other papers.

Adjourned.

Voted to authorize the Home Dairy Test Committee to make the awards after the year has expired and to give orders on the Treasurer for the premiums.

Voted to make the Home Dairy Test a permanent institution of the Association.

SCALE OF POINTS.

As Suggested by a Joint Committee from the United States and Canada Ayrshire Breeders' Association.

Scale of Points for Ayrshire Bull.

Head	16
Forehead—Broad and clearly defined...... 2	
Horn—Strong at base, set wide apart inclining upward 1	
Face—Of medium length, clean cut, showing facial veins 2	
Muzzle—Broad and strong without coarseness 1	
Nostrils—Large and open 2	
Jaws—Wide at the base and strong........ 1	
Eyes—Moderately large, full and bright.... 3	
Ears—Of medium size and fine, carried alert 1	
Expression—Full of vigor, resolution and masculinity 3	
NECK—Of medium length, somewhat arched, large and strong in the muscles on top, inclined to flatness on sides, enlarging symmetrically towards the shoulders, throat clean and free from loose skin	10
FOREQUARTERS	15
Shoulders—Strong, smoothly blending into body, with good distance through from point to point and fine on top............ 3	
Chest—Low, deep and full between and back of forelegs 8	
Brisket—Deep, not too prominent and with very little dewlap...................... 2	

Legs and Feet—Legs well apart, straight and short, shanks fine and smooth, joints firm, feet of medium size, round, solid and deep 2

BODY 18
Back—Short and straight, chine strongly developed and open-jointed 5
Loin—Broad, strong and level 4
Ribs—Long, broad, strong, well sprung and wide apart 4
Abdomen—Large and deep, trimly held up with muscular development 4
Flank—Thin and arching 1

HINDQUARTERS 16
Rump—Level, long from hooks to pin bones, 5
Hooks—Medium distance apart, proportionately narrower than in female, not rising above the level of the back 2
Pin Bones—High, wide apart 2
Thighs—Thin, long and wide apart 4
Tail—Fine, long and set on a level with back 1
Legs and Feet—Legs straight, set well apart, shanks fine and smooth; feet medium size, round, solid and deep, not to cross in walking 2

SCROTUM—Well developed and strongly carried.. 3
Rudimentaries, Veins, etc. Teats of uniform size, squarely placed, wide apart and free from scrotum; veins long, large, tortuous, with extensions entering large orifices; escutcheon pronounced and covering a large surface 4

COLOR—Red of any shade, brown or these with white, mahogany and white, or white; each color distinctly defined 3

COVERING 6
   Skin—Medium thickness, mellow and elastic 3
   Hair—Soft and fine 2
   Secretions—Oily, of rich brown or yellow color 1

STYLE—Active, vigorous, showing strong masculine character, temperament inclined to nervousness but not irritable or vicious......... 5

WEIGHT at maturity not less than 1,500 pounds.. 4

Total 100

Scale of Points for Ayrshire Cow.

HEAD 10
   Forehead—Broad and clearly defined...... 1
   Horns—Wide set on and inclining upward.. 1
   Face—Of medium length, slightly dished, clean cut, showing veins 2
   Muzzle—Broad and strong without coarseness, nostrils large 1
   Jaws—Wide at the base and strong......... 1
   Eyes—Full and bright with placid expression 3
   Ears—Of medium size and fine, carried alert 1

NECK—Fine throughout, throat clean, neatly jointed to head and shoulders, of good length, moderately thin, nearly free from loose skin, elegant in bearing........................... 3

FOREQUARTERS 10
    Shoulders—Light, good distance through from point to point but sharp at withers, smoothly blending into body............ 2
    Chest—Low, deep and full between and back of forelegs 6
    Brisket—Light 1
    Legs and Feet—Legs straight and short, well apart, shanks fine and smooth, joints firm; feet medium size, round, solid and deep 1

BODY 13
    Back—Strong and straight, chine lean, sharp and open-jointed 4
    Loin—Broad, strong and level............. 2
    Ribs—Long, broad, wide apart and well sprung 3
    Abdomen—Capacious, deep, firmly held up with strong muscular development........ 3
    Flank—Thin and arching................. 1

HINDQUARTERS 11
    Rump—Wide, level and long from hooks to pin bones, a reasonable pelvic arch allowed 3
    Hooks—Wide apart and not projecting above back nor unduly overlaid with fat........ 2
    Pin Bones—High and wide apart.......... 1
    Thighs—Thin, long and wide apart........ 2
    Tail—Long, fine, set on a level with the back 1
    Legs and Feet—Legs strong, short, straight when viewed from behind and set well apart; shanks fine and smooth, joints firm; feet medium size, round solid and deep.... 2

UDDER—Long, wide, deep but not pendulous, nor fleshy; firmly attached to the body, extending well up behind and far forward; quarters even; sole nearly level and not indented between teats, udder veins well developed and plainly visible.................. 22

TEATS—Evenly placed, distance apart from side to side equal to half the breadth of udder, from back to front equal to one-third the length; length 2 1-2 to 3 1-2 inches, thickness in keeping with length, hanging perpendicular and not tapering......................... 8

MAMMARY VEINS—Large, long, tortuous branching and entering large orifices.......... 5

ESCUTCHEON—Distinctly defined, spreading over thighs and extending well upward........ 2

COLOR—Red of any shade, brown or these with white; mahogany and white, or white; each color distinctly defined. (Brindle markings allowed but not desirable).................... 2

COVERING 6
   Skin—Of medium thickness, mellow and elastic 3
   Hair—Soft and fine..................... 2
   Secretions—Oily, of rich brown or yellow color 1

STYLE—Alert, vigorous, showing strong character; temperament inclined to nervousness but still docile............................. 4

WEIGHT at maturity not less than one thousand pounds 4

    Total........................... 100

CHARTER.

An Act to Incorporate the Ayrshire Breeders' Association.

It is hereby enacted by the General Assembly of the State of Vermont:

Sec. 1. J. D. W. French, James F. Converse, Alonzo Libby, F. H. Mason, Obadiah Brown, Henry E. Smith, C. M. Winslow, S. M. Wells, H. R. C. Watson, James Scott, George A. Fletcher, Charles H. Hayes, John Stewart, their associates and successors, are constituted a body corporate by the name of the "Ayrshire Breeders' Association," and by that name may sue and be sued; may acquire by gift or purchase, hold and convey real and personal estate necessary for the purposes of this corporation, not to exceed twenty-five thousand dollars; may have a common seal and alter the same at pleasure.

Sec. 2. The object of this corporation shall be to publish a Herd Book, and for such other purposes as may be conducive to the interests of breeders of Ayrshire cattle.

Sec. 3. This corporation may elect officers and make such by-laws, rules and regulations for the management of its business as may be necessary, not inconsistent with the laws of this State.

Sec. 4. This corporation may hold its meetings at such time and place as the corporation may appoint.

Sec. 5. This act shall take effect from its passage.

JOSIAH GROUT,
Speaker of the House of Representatives.

LEVI K. FULLER,
President of the Senate.

Approved November 23, 1886.

EBENEZER J. ORMSBEE,
Governor.

(A true copy).

Attest: E. W. J. Hawkins, Engrossing Clerk.

CONSTITUTION.

PREAMBLE.

We, the undersigned breeders of Ayrshire cattle, recognizing the importance of a trustworthy Herd Book that shall be accepted as a final authority in all questions of pedigree, and desiring to secure the co-operation of all who feel an interest in preserving the purity of this stock, do hereby agree to form an Association for the publication of a Herd Book, and for such other purposes as may be conducive to the interests of breeders, and adopt the following Constitution:

ARTICLE I.

This Association shall be called the Ayrshire Breeders' Association.

ARTICLE II.

The members of the Association shall comprise only the original signers of this Constitution, and such other persons as may be admitted, as hereinafter provided.

ARTICLE III.

SEC. I. The officers of the Association shall consist of a President, four Vice-Presidents, a Treasurer, a Secretary and an Auditor, who together with six members of the Association, all chosen by ballot, shall constitute an Executive Committee.

SEC. 2. The President, Secretary and Treasurer shall be the Finance Committee ex officio.

SEC. 3. The President, Vice-Presidents, Treasurer, Secretary and Auditor shall be elected annually.

The six members who make up the balance of the Executive Committee shall be elected as follows: Two members for one year, two members for two years and two members for three years, and hereafter two members shall be elected each year for a term of three years.

SEC. 4. The President shall preside at all meetings of the members of the Association, and all meetings of the Executive Committee when he is present, but when absent a Vice-President shall act in his stead. The President shall sign all Certificates of Membership which may be issued, and shall be the custodian of all bonds given by officers of the Association, or renewals thereof.

SEC. 5. The Finance Committee shall have authority to take the entire control and management of the affairs of the Association, between the Annual Meetings, with full power and authority to do what they deem proper and best for its interests, but nothing contrary to the expressed wish of the Association.

SEC. 6. The Treasurer shall have charge of all the funds of the Association and make all investments thereof, subject to the provisions of the section regulating the Finance Committee, and shall pay all bills of the Association, after being indorsed by the Finance Committee and approved by the Auditor, and shall perform such other duties as are incident to the office of Treasurer.

He shall give a bond with sureties, to the satisfaction of the Finance Committee and Auditor.

SEC. 7. The Secretary shall be the corresponding and recording officer of the Association, shall sign and issue all certificates of membership and registry and of transfer registry, and shall keep a record of all such certificates issued, and do such other duties as are incident to the office of Secretary.

He shall edit and publish the Herd Book at such times and in such form as the Executive Committee may direct.

He is authorized to expend such sums as he may find necessary for the carrying on the ordinary business of his office, and shall keep an accurate account in detail of all moneys received and paid out by him in the performance of his duties, a copy of which he shall transmit quarterly, during the week next succeeding the quarter, to the Auditor, and shall at the same time send to the Treasurer whatever moneys he may have on hand at the ending of the quarter.

He shall give a bond with sureties to the satisfaction of the Finance Committee and Auditor.

Sec. 8. The Finance Committee shall annually examine the condition of the Association in its financial and business affairs, and report its condition to the Association at its Annual Meeting, and in conjunction with the Treasurer shall act in making investments of the funds of the Association.

Any disagreement between the Finance Committee as to the investment or care of the funds of the Association shall be referred to the Executive Committee for final adjustment.

All bills against the Association shall be approved by the Finance Committee and sent by them to the Auditor.

Sec. 9. The Auditor shall examine all accounts sent him from any member of the Finance Committee, and if found correct, shall approve and forward the same to the Treasurer for payment, and shall annually, when auditing the accounts of the year for the Secretary and Treasurer, previous to the Annual Meeting, make a complete inventory of all property found in the hands of the Secretary and Treasurer, and forward the same to the Finance Committee, which shall be incorporated in the report of the Finance Committee to the Association at their Annual Meeting.

Sec. 10. The Treasurer, Secretary and Auditor shall receive such compensation for their services as the Association shall determine.

Article IV.

The Annual Meeting of the Association shall be held each year at such time and place as shall be designated by the Executive Committee (of which notice shall be sent to members at least one month previous) for the discussion of questions of interest to the members, and for the election of officers for the ensuing year. Special meetings of the Association may be called by the President or by the Executive Committee, or at the written request of ten members. Twenty days' notice must be given and the object of the meeting announced in the call, and no business other than that specified in the call shall be transacted at the special meeting. Time and place shall be determined in same way as Annual Meeting.

At all meetings of the Association members may vote in person or by proxy, or they may send their ballot by mail to the Secretary, whose duty it shall be to vote the same, and to acknowledge their receipt. At least twenty members present, represented by proxy or written ballot, shall be a quorum for transacting business.

Article V.

Only breeders of Ayrshire cattle shall be eligible for membership, and members shall be elected at any regular meeting of the Association; also by the unanimous written consent of the Executive Committee at any time between the annual meetings, subject to the following conditions:

Each applicant for membership shall be recommended by one or more members of the Association as a trustworthy and careful breeder; and no new member shall be admitted if objected to by any officer of the Association.

The Secretary shall notify the candidate of his rejection, or, in case of his election, that he will be admitted as a member on signing the Constitution and paying the initiation fee.

An applicant who has been rejected shall not be voted on again until two years from the date of his rejection, unless by the unanimous consent of the officers of the Association.

Article VI.

Each member shall pay an initiation fee of twenty-five dollars. These fees shall constitute an Association fund to defray the expenses of publishing the Herd Book, and other charges incidental to the organization of the Association, and to the transaction of its business.

No officer or member shall be authorized to contract any debt in the name of the Association.

Article VII.

The Herd Book shall be edited by an editor appointed for that purpose under the control and supervision of the Executive Committee, and shall be published only with its official approval.

The charge for entry of the pedigree of each animal belonging to a member of the Association shall be fixed by the Executive Committee, but shall not exceed one dollar, except for an animal two years old.

Animals not belonging to members of the Association may be entered in the Herd Book upon the payment of twice the amount charged to members.

The Herd Book charges shall be appropriated to the examination and verification of pedigrees and the preparation of the Herd Book, which shall be published by the Association and be its property. The price of the Herd Book shall be determined by the Executive Committee. The editor shall keep on file all documents constituting his authority for pedigrees, and shall hold them subject to the inspection of any member of the Association, and shall deliver them to his successor in office.

Article VIII.

Should it occur at any time that any member of the Association shall be charged with wilful misrepresentation in regard to any animal, or with any other act derogatory to the standing of the Association, the Executive Committee shall examine into the matter; and, if it shall find there is foundation for such a charge, the offending member may be expelled by a vote of two-thirds of the members of the Association present or represented at any regular meeting.

Article IX.

This Constitution may be altered or amended by a vote of two-thirds of the members present or represented by proxy at any annual meeting of the Association.

Notice of proposed alterations or amendments shall be given in the call for said meeting.

REGULATIONS.

1. Only such animals shall be admitted to the Herd Book as are proved to be either imported from Scotland, or descended from such imported animals.

2. All animals hereafter imported to be eligible to registry in the Ayrshire Record must previously be recorded in the Ayrshire Herd Book of Scotland, and an application for registry must be accompanied by a certificate of registry duly signed by the Secretary in Scotland.

Entries of calves imported in dam must be accompanied by the certificate of registry of sire and dam in the Scotch Herd Book, also certificate of bull service signed by owner of bull.

3. No animal not already named and entered in some Herd Book shall be accepted for entry under a name that

has already been offered for entry; also, the affix 1st, 2d and 3d shall apply only to calves of the cow bearing the name used; not to her grandchildren or any other animal.

4. The breeder of an animal shall be considered the one owning the dam at the time of her service by the bull.

5. No pedigree will be received for entry from any one, except the breeder of the animal offered, unless it is accompanied by a certificate of the breeder or his legal representative, indorsing the pedigree.

Entries of calves, sired by bulls not owned by the breeder of the calf, shall be accompanied by a certificate of bull service signed by owner of bull.

6. All animals sold, in order that their progeny may be registered, must have their successive transfers duly recorded. Records of transfers will be made only on the certificate of former owner, or his legal representative.

7. A transfer-book shall be kept by the Editor, in which all changes of ownership shall be recorded.

8. The Editor shall keep a record of the deaths of all animals which may be sent to him. (And breeders are requested to forward the same, stating cause, etc.)

9. The fees for recording are one dollar for each animal recorded by and in the name of a member of the Association, being either bred or owned by him, and two dollars for animals over two years old at the time of entry, but this is not intended to allow at members' rates, the recording of calves born after the dam is sold, when the owner is not a member.

On imported animals the two-year limit is reckoned from the date of importation, and the same on animals brought from Canada.

A fee of twenty-five cents will be charged for recording ancestors necessary to complete a pedigree to importation or to cattle already in the Ayrshire Record, when the record is for cattle bred and owned by other parties, and is of no other value to the person having the recording done, other than to admit his animal to record.

Transfer fee twenty-five cents.

Double the above rates are charged to those not members.

Duplicate certificates of entry or transfer twenty-five cents each.

A fee of fifty cents will be charged for a Custom House certificate on each animal imported from Canada.

All the above fees should accompany the entry or transfer papers to insure attention.

10. An individual membership shall be continued after the death of a member in the settlement of his estate until the same shall be settled, and then the membership shall cease. The inheritor of a herd of Ayrshires shall also inherit the membership of the Ayrshire Breeders' Association—subject to approval of said Association. In case of corporations, the corporation may continue as a member so long as they are interested in the Association, and shall be represented by such person as may be designated by the President and Secretary of the corporation.

The surviving member of a firm may be the member of the Association.

A firm shall have but one address.

11. These Regulations may be altered, amended or added to, with the consent of two-thirds of the officers of the Association and Executive Committee.

GENERAL INFORMATION.

Each volume of the Ayrshire Record, I to XVIII, inclusive, may be obtained of the Treasurer, N. S. Winsor, Greenville, R. I., postage paid, $2.25.

Milk record blanks to accommodate herds of thirty-three cows may be had of the Secretary, C. M. Winslow, Brandon, Vt., $1.50 per 100.

Blanks for extending Pedigrees to five generations may be had of the Secretary at $1.00 per 100, postage paid.

Private Herd Book records, board cover, may be had of the Secretary at $1.50 each, postage paid, arranged for tabulated pedigree for seventy-five (75) cows, with spaces for monthly milk and butter record for eight years, service and produce record for twelve years.

All blanks necessary for recording and transferring Ayrshires may be had of the Secretary free of charge.

Membership fee $25.00, which is for life, not transferable, and no assessments.

The survivor of a partnership may become the member.

The inheritor of a herd may also inherit the membership.

The partnership of a herd can apply to only one herd and cannot be divided for two herds or in two post-office addresses.

Members' fees for recording, $1.00 for each animal under two years old, $2.00 for each animal over two years old.

The date of the two-year limit in age is reckoned from the date the application for record is mailed.

The two-year limit on animals imported or brought from Canada is reckoned from date of Custom House receipt.

Transfer fee, twenty-five cents.

A fee of twenty-five cents each is charged for recording ancestors necessary to complete a pedigree to importation, or to cattle already recorded in the Ayrshire Record when the record is for cattle bred and owned by other parties and is of no other value to the person recording

Double the above rates to non-members.

The rate charged is governed by the fact of whether the person sending the application is a member or non-member, and not by who bred the animal.

Duplicate certificates of entry or transfer, twenty-five cents each.

A charge of $1.00 each is made for investigating a Canadian pedigree to learn its eligibility to record, which will be applied towards the recording if the animal is to be recorded.

A fee of fifty cents each is charged for a Custom House certificate for animals imported from Canada.

By mutual agreement of the "Canadian Ayrshire Herd Book Association" and "Ayrshire Breeders' Association" entries from the Canadian Herd Book of animals that are sold to parties in the United States and are found to be eligible to entry in the Ayrshire Record, will be received from the Canadians at the following rates for entry regardless of any age limit: One dollar for the animal presented for record, and $1.00 each for the ancestors to the number of ten, and twenty-five cents for each ancestor back of ten in number necessary to connect to animals already registered in the Ayrshire Record or to importation from Scotland.

Application for entry of Canadian bred animals owned by non-members of the Ayrshire Breeders' Association will have to be accompanied with a Canadian certificate of entry as authority for accepting the pedigree.

No animal will be received for record that does not trace in each branch of its pedigree step by step by name and number to a reliable importation.

All the above fees should accompany the applications to insure attention.

In giving sire and dam be careful to always give the Herd Book number of sire and dam.

When purchasing an animal be sure to get a transfer or see that the seller sends one to the Secretary for record.

When buying a female in calf be sure to get a certificate of bull service from the owner of the cow, and attach it to the application for entry of her calf when sending in for record.

In filling out an application for entry of an animal that is sold there is no need of a separate transfer, but enter it in the line for owner with date of sale, and there is no extra charge for a transfer when so recorded.

In giving the markings on the back of the application blank be careful to mark with ink and as accurately as possible, marking *r* for the red spots and *w* for the white spots.

When buying Ayrshires in Canada our Government admits free of duty if they are registered in our book before being entered at the Custom House, and it is much safer not to move them from the owner until they are recorded, because sometimes it happens that the pedigree must be looked up at the Canada office, and there is often considerable delay. Then, too, there are some animals recorded in the Canadian Books that are not eligible to record in ours, and if they are recorded in our books before closing the trade, it saves loss to buyer.

Sometimes buyers go into Canada and are persuaded to buy and pay the duty to save time, but this is risky, as afterwards it is sometimes found that such animals cannot be recorded in our book.

The Canadians sometimes try to convince the buyer that it is just as well to simply continue the Canada Register, and record there instead of in our book, which is not true, as a record in the Canada book is only valuable in Canada. All Ayrshires to be salable this side the line must be recorded in our book or be eligible to such record.

It would be wise for any one having an Ayrshire cow of extraordinary dairy ability to have her tested for Advanced Registry.

RULES FOR ADVANCED REGISTRY.

PREAMBLE.

For the purpose of encouraging a better system of keeping milk and butter records, and that we may obtain more reliable records of the dairy yield of Ayrshire cows, we hereby adopt the following rules and regulations for the establishment of a system of Advanced Registry for Ayrshire cattle:

RULE I.

The Secretary of the Association shall have charge of the registry under the general supervision and direction of the Executive Committee, shall prepare and publish blank forms and circulars needed in carrying this system into effect, receive and attend to all applications for this registry, and have general oversight and direction of all official tests of all milk and butter production for it, and perform such other duties as may be required to secure the efficiency and success of this system. He shall make a full report of his work in this branch at the annual meeting each year, and publish the entries when so ordered by the Executive Committee.

RULE II.

All tests shall be for a period of 365 consecutive days.

RULE III.

CLASSIFICATION OF ANIMALS.

Cows from two to three years old shall be in a class known as the two-year-old form.

Cows from three to four years old shall be in a class known as the three-year-old form.

Cows from four to five years old shall be in a class known as the four-year-old form.

Cows above five years old shall be in a class known as the full-age form.

RULE IV.

ELIGIBILITY OF BULLS.

No bull shall be eligible to Advanced Registry unless he shall have been previously recorded in the Ayrshire record.

a A bull to be eligible to advanced registry shall be a typical Ayrshire bull in general appearance, shall scale 80 points and have two daughters in the Registry from different dams.

b A bull may be admitted to Advanced Registry without physical qualifications, and without scaling, provided he has four daughters in the Advanced Registry from different dams.

RULE V.

ELIGIBILITY OF COWS.

No cow shall be admitted to Advanced Registry unless she shall have been previously recorded in the Ayrshire Record.

TWO-YEAR-OLD FORM.

Year's record. If her record begins the day she is two years old, or before that time, she shall, to entitle her to record, give not less than 6,000 pounds of milk in 365 consecutive days from the beginning of the test and 214.3 pounds of butter fat, and for each day she is over two years old at time of beginning the test there shall be added 1.37 pounds of milk to the 6,000 pounds and .06 pounds of butter fat to the 214.3 pounds.

THREE YEAR OLD FORM.

If her record begins the day she is three years old, she shall, to entitle her to record, give not less than 6,500 pounds of milk in 365 consecutive days from the beginning of the test and 236 pounds of butter fat, and for each day she is over three years old at the time of beginning the test there shall be added 2.74 pounds of milk to the 6,500 pounds and .12 pounds of butter fat to the 236 pounds, which addition shall be made in each succeeding form to maturity.

FOUR YEAR OLD FORM.

Year's record—7,500 pounds of milk and 279 pounds of butter fat.

MATURE FORM

Year's record—8,500 pounds of milk and 322 pounds of butter fat.

RULE VI.

PERIOD FOR MAKING TESTS.

All tests for a year shall be commenced as soon after calving as practicable, and shall not extend beyond 365 days from the commencement of the test, and in no case shall the test include the milk or butter fat from a second calving.

RULE VII.

APPLICATION FOR TESTS.

An application for a test will not be accepted from a person who is not a member of the Ayrshire Breeders' Association. Application for intended tests should be made to the Secretary as long as possible before the desired time for beginning such tests in order to allow sufficient time to arrange with the Experiment Station of the state where the owner is located for their supervision of the test.

In making application for a test, the owner should give sufficient evidence of the capability of the cow to qualify to warrant making the test.

RULE VIII.

METHOD OF CONDUCTING TESTS.

All tests shall be under the supervision of the Secretary and the Experiment Station of the state where the test is being made, or such persons as may be appointed by concurrence of Secretary and Station.

The owner shall weigh each milking from each cow being tested and keep a careful record of the same on blank forms furnished by the Secretary, and at the end of each month he shall add the amount of milk given by each cow and set it down in the column prepared for that purpose, and send the filled blank to the Secretary as soon as possible after the month is ended.

In addition to this, the Experiment Station will send an agent to the stable each month, to make a two days' test of the milk of each cow in the test, for quantity given at each milking during his visit and for the amount of butter fat in each sample.

He will also inspect the method of weighing and the daily record, compare the weights with those given during his visit and report the same to the Secretary. The milk record kept by the owner of the cows being tested will be accepted as the record for the year, provided it agrees practically with that taken monthly by the agent.

The result of each cow's test shall be computed in the following manner: The weights of milk produced each month shall be multiplied by the per cent of butter fat as shown by the official test for that month.

If it is desired to show the amount of commercial butter, it shall be obtained by the Experiment Station method of the addition of one sixth, being on a basis of 85 per cent fat.

RULE IX.

All the expense incurred by the Association in the employment of the Experiment Station or their agent in conducting the test shall be divided equally between the Association and the member having the test made. It is expected that the member having the test made will without charge render such assistance as he is able to the agent, in conveyance to the railroad station and in entertainment while making the monthly test.

RULE X.

NO FEE REQUIRED FOR ENTRIES.

In view of the public benefits accruing from investigations under this system of registry, and of personal benefits to owners and breeders of Ayrshire cattle from demonstrations of their superiority by properly authenticated milk and butter records made, gathered and preserved through this system, no fees will be charged for any form of entry in its Register.

RULE XI.

AMENDMENT.

These rules may be altered, amended or added to by a two-thirds vote of the members present at any regular meeting of the Association, notice of proposed amendment having been given in the call for said meeting.

HOME DAIRY TEST 1908.

PRIZES FOR BUTTER FAT.

The Ayrshire Breeders' Association offers the following premiums for cows or herds of Ayrshires making the best records for butter fat for one year under the conditions hereafter named.

FOR INDIVIDUAL COWS $30.00, $20.00, $10.00.

FOR HERDS OF FIVE COWS EACH $75.00, $50.00, $25.00.

SPECIAL SILVER CUP PRIZE.

In addition to the above cash prizes we are pleased to offer a piece of silver plate obtained from the income of the "French Fund" of $1,500.00 donated by Miss Cornelia A. French, North Andover, Mass., in memory of her brother, the late J. D. W. French, and offered for the herd of five cows which shall give the largest record for a year, of milk and butter fat, beginning April 1st.

The special award shall be based on a uniform scale of points as follows:

For every pound of milk given by the five cows, 1 point.

For every pound of butter fat given by the five cows, 17 1-2 points.

CONDITIONS OF TEST.

OPEN TO MEMBERS OF THE AYRSHIRE BREEDERS' ASSOCIATION ONLY.

1. All animals competing must be registered in the Ayrshire Record and stand on the books of the Association as owned by the person competing.

2. The year's test will commence April 1st, 1908, and notice of proposed entry to tests must be sent to the Secretary of the Association not later than March 15th, so as to allow time for arrangements for tests to begin April 1st, 1908.

3. Each contestant shall name from five to twelve cows or heifers to be tested through the year, and at

the end of the year he may select any three of these for the individual cow prizes and any five for the herd prizes, but shall not select the same cow for both individual and herd prizes nor shall he be allowed to duplicate entries, nor shall he enter the same herd or single cow for both Home Dairy Test prizes and the special prize, but may choose at the end of the year where he will enter his herd or single cows, for any of the prizes, Home Dairy or Special.

4. At the end of each month every contestant shall report to the Secretary of the Association, upon blanks furnished them for such purpose by such office:

a A complete record of weights of each milking with the correct footing of each for the month.

b The calving and service record for that month.

c An approximate statement of the amount and kind of food given the animals, the manner of stabling and care of same, a full statement for the first month, and after that enter on the blank for that month any changes in food or care as they occur from month to month during the year.

5 These tests shall be under the supervision of the Committee appointed by the Ayrshire Breeders' Association, but any member of the committee owning animals competing in said tests shall be barred from having supervision of his own test or tests, but some other member of the committee may supervise and take charge of the test. All cows shall be wholly under the control of the owner, so far as feeding and general treatment are concerned.

6 All tests shall be under the supervision of the Committee and the Experiment Station of the state where the herd being tested is located. In order to save expense and insure careful supervision, arrangements will be

made as far as possible to secure the services of Experiment Station Agents living not too far from the herd being tested.

7. The Experiment Station will send an Agent monthly to make a two days' test of the milk from each cow in the test, and to compare the weights of the daily milkings with those the Agent makes for the two days he is present.

8. The sampling of milk and sending the same to the Experiment Station will be done by the Experiment Station Agent.

9 The daily weights of milk made by the Contestant will be accepted, provided they do not materially differ from the weights taken by the Agent at his monthly visits.

10. The result of each year's test shall be computed in the following manner: The weights of milk produced each month shall be multiplied by the per cent. of butter fat as shown by the official test for that month, and the sum of the results thus obtained shall be the year's record. The milk will also be tested for per cent. of total solids, but this, however, will not be considered in making the awards, which will be on amount of butter fat only.

The expense incurred from employing the Experiment Station shall be equally divided between the Contestant and the Association. It is expected that the Contestant will convey the Experiment Station Agent to and from the railroad station and entertain him while making the tests free of charge.

Testing for advanced registry can be made in connection with the Home Dairy Test with no extra expense, and it is advisable to carry along the two at the same time.

    C. M. WINSLOW,
    THOMAS TURNBULL, Jr.,
    W. V. PROBASCO,
        Committee on Home Dairy Tests.

EXPERT JUDGES AT FAIRS.

The result of the nomination of expert judges by the special committee, to be endorsed by the Executive Committee, is the appointment of F. W. Spalding, Poultney, Vermont, as the Expert Judge of Ayrshires for the season of 1908.

OFFICERS OF THE ASSOCIATION.

President.
E. J. Fletcher....................Greenfield, N. H.

Vice-Presidents.
George E. Pike....................Gouverneur, N. Y.
George H. McFadden................Bryn Mawr, Pa.
Elmer F. Pember.....................Bangor, Me.
J. F. Converse....................Woodville, N. Y.

Secretary and Editor.
C. M. Winslow.......................Brandon, Vt.

Treasurer.
N. S. Winsor........................Greenville, R. I.

Auditor.
George H. Yeaton....................Dover, N. H.

Balance of Executive Committee.
Charles H. Hayes......Portsmouth, N. H., for 3 years
John W. Oakey.........Bryn Mawr, Pa., for 3 years
John R. Valentine........Bryn Mawr, Pa., for 2 years
L. A. Reymann........Wheeling, W. Va., for 2 years
Howard Cook................Beloit, Ohio, for 1 year
W. P. Schanck................Avon, N. Y., for 1 year

MEMBERS OF THE ASSOCIATION.

CALIFORNIA.
Bement, George..........................Fruitvale

COLORADO.

Osgood, J. C..............................Redstone

CONNECTICUT.

Aiken, Ella R........................Norwalk, Conn.
Baton, John A. & Son.....................Wauregan
Connecticut Agricultural College...............Storrs
'onnecticut Insane Asylum...............Middletown
Dorrance, Henry...........................Plainfield
Ennis, Alfred A...........................Danielson
Fischer, W. H............................New Canaan
Greene, B. D..............................Stamford
Kahn, George A..............................Yantic
Larned, J. H................................Putnam
Manwaring, John............................Norwich
Palmer, Edward G.........................Plainfield
Roode, Joseph..........................Jewett City
Sears, N. E................................Elmwood
Weed, John W..............................Noroton
Wells, Dudley.........................Wethersfield
Wells, Dudley, 2d.....................Wethersfield
Wells, William T........................Newington

ILLINOIS.

Crabb, Frank A...........................Litchfield
Jones, Granville.........................Galesburgh
Stewart, John...............................Elburn

INDIANA.

Richards, C. C.......................Malotte Park

KANSAS.

Delap, S. N...................................Iola

MAINE.

Bearce, George B..........................Lewiston
Buckley, J. P..........................Stroudwater
Burnham, M. M..................Cumberland Centre

Dearborne, A. J.....................West Falmouth
Good Will Home Association................Hinckley
Hunnewell, A. A....................New Gloucester
Hunt, H. C..............................Brunswick
Ness, John A. & Rowland....................Auburn
Pember, Elmer F...........................Bangor

Maryland.

Harrison, Charles K.....................Pikesville
Scott, J. McPherson....................Hagerstown

Massachusetts.

Bacon, P. K..............................Campello
Barnes, B. F............................Haverhill
Beldon, C. M.........................South Natick
Boise, Enos W...........................Blandford
Bowker, George H........................Westboro
Burt, Jairus F.......................Easthampton
Choate, Charles F.......................Southboro
Clark, Franklin P........................Sudbury
Cooke, F. C..............................Carlisle
Copeland, Davis & Son....................Campello
Crissey, Warren..................Great Barrington
Curtis, L. W........................Globe Village
Doe, Charles C..........................Lexington
Easterbrook Brothers......................Webster
French, C. A........................North Andover
Hamilton Woolen Co....................Southbridge
Harrington, H. A........................Worcester
Haskell, A. M.......................North Beverly
Heath, G. P............................Northboro
Knowlton, George W....................West Upton
Lawrence, James...........................Groton
Leach, J. Hooper......................Bridgewater
Leach, Philo..........................Bridgewater
Merriam, Herbert...........................Weston
Marsh, William H.....................Barre Plains

Morrell, Harry E..........................Wayland
Mt. Hermon Boys' School................Mt. Hermon
Peirce, F. C......................Concord Junction
Perley, Charles...........................Bradford
Pierce, George H..........................Concord
Piper, Anson C........................South Acton
Reed, Hammon............................Lexington
Sage, Charles D....................North Brookfield
Scott, Thaxter & Son.......................Hawley
Smith, Peter D............................Andover
Stevens, Edmund H......................Cambridge
Stone, George F..........................Littleton
Thorp, John C.............................Holyoke
Tyler, Arthur F.............................Athol
Walker, William I.................Great Barrington
Young, Gilman P...........................Grafton

Michigan.
Michigan School for the Deaf.................Flint

Minnesota.
Hill, James J.............................St. Paul
Reeve, C. McC.........................Minneapolis
Scott, John W..............................Austin
Wilcox, John F........................Minneapolis

Mississippi.
Surget, James.............................Natchez

Missouri.
University of Missouri....................Columbia

Montana.
Davidson, E. M. & Son.....................Bozeman

New Hampshire.
Abbott, J. N..............................Concord
Bell, Charles J.............................Hollis

Breck, Stephen R.	Claremont
Cater, H. F. & Son	North Barrington
Childs, Harlow N.	Piermont
Clark, George C.	Orford
Cross, W. L.	Ponemah
Edes, Samuel	Newport
Fletcher, Etna J.	South Lyndeboro
Garvin, W. R.	Dover
Hayes, Charles H.	Portsmouth
Hayes, Charles S.	Portsmouth
Holt, Andy	Lyndeboro
Holt, E. A.	Hudson
Kimball, Herbert M.	Concord
Marshall, William C.	Laconia
Rockwood, C. E. & Son	Temple
Russell, Frank E.	Greenfield
Sawyer, E. E.	Atkinson
Strafford County Farm	Dover
The Uplands	Bridgewater
Upham, Charles H. & Son	Thornton's Ferry
Yeaton, George H.	Dover

New Jersey.

Beach, Frederick H.	Dover
Burke, Joseph F.	Morristown
Casterline, J. Andrew	Dover
Crane, John	Union
Farley, F. C.	Milburn
Freeman, Charles D.	Iselin
Glen Alpine Farm	Morristown
Lindsay, William	Plainfield
Magie, J. D. & B. P.	Elizabeth
Probasco, W. V.	Cream Ridge
Sadler, Edward W.	Montclair

Tilton, E. A.................................Hamilton
Whittingham, W. R........................Milburn

NEW YORK.

Arden Farms Dairy Co., Wm. Viner, Sup't......Arden
Ashley, E. L..............................Glens Falls
Babcock, F. M.............................Gouverneur
Ballou, George William...................Middletown
Barnes, N...............................Middle Hope
Barney, C. S...............................Milford
Barney, Kent ....Milford
Bell, George H................................Rome
Brayton, C. N..........................South Wales
Burdick, George W.......................Friendship
Burdick, Thomas J. & Sons....................Alfred
Button, E. L...............................Melrose
Buttrick, C. A..........................Liberty Falls
Campbell, John S.....................New York Mills
Clark, C. W..............................Guymard
Clark, N. E...............................Potsdam
Colburn, J. L..............................Milford
Conger, Lawton M...........................Collins
Converse, J. F...........................Woodville
Cookingham, F. H.......................Cherry Creek
Crowley, Thomas J.........................Potsdam
Delaney, J. J............................Grindstone
Doane, Franklin..........................Middletown
Dorn, Elmer J............................Johnstown
Dunham, Lawrence,......260 Columbus Ave., New York
Emery, C. G...............................Clayton
Griffin, J. H................................Moira
Guernsey, James H. & Co..................Woodhull
Hall, Lott...............................Gouverneur
Ham, Eugene...............................Verbank
Hamilton, William Pierson................Sterlington

Harrington, A. D.................................Oxford
Hatch, C. E...................................Gainesville
Hawkes, E. B................................Wells Bridge
Hill, J. Edwin & Son.........................Gouverneur
Hillman, A. E. & Son..............................Cuyler
Horton, H. A.....................................Johnson
Howatt, Gerald...............................White Plains
Hubbard, George D................................Camden
Huffstater, L................................Sandy Creek
Hulett, H. L..................................Allentown
Hyde, J. B..................120 Broadway, New York
Jackson, B. O. & Son...........................Boonville
Jay, William.....................................Katonah
Jenkins, J. W....................................Vernon
Karr, S. S. & Sons...............................Almond
Kenyon, Louis H...................................Utopia
Lansing, E. TenEyck.........................Little Falls
Leach, J. S. & Son............................Gouverneur
Lewis, C. W. & Sons.......................Alfred Station
Litchard, A. L. & Son..........................Rushford
McCrea, Robert................................Champlain
Mercereau, W. W. & H. B..........................Vestal
Nichols, James H.................................Carmel
Norton, W. H....................................Belmont
Oneida Community, Limited......................Kenway
Ormiston Brothers..................................Cuba
Paget, A. H...................................Lakeville
Pike, George E...............................Gouverneur
Ramsdell, H. S..................................Newburgh
Rhodes, T. F...................................Camillus
Ricker, Clarence.................................Belmont
Rogers, G. L.................................Gouverneur
Ryder, Arthur B..............................Barnerville
Schanck, W. P......................................Avon
Schouten, E. A..................................Cortland

Sears, B. C.............................Blooming Grove
Siver, D. E...............................Cooperstown
Skinner, Harry W...............................Utica
Smith, Oliver & Son.......................Chateaugay
Stetson, Francis Lynde.....................Sterlington
Story, S. S..........................North Stockholm
Stowell, L. D. & Sons.......................Black Creek
Stowell, W. C..............................Black Creek
Strickland, J. P...........................Cattaraugus
Taber, George............................East Aurora
Taylor, John L..................................Owego
Tod, Wm. Stewart..........45 Wall Street, New York
Topping, R. R..............................Amsterdam
Tubbs, Ambie S...........................Maple View
Tucker, W. G..............................Elm Valley
Tuttle, M. A............................Hornellsville
Underhill, C. S..............................Glenham
Verplank, Samuel ....Fishkill-on-Hudson
Ward, M. J..................................Treadwell
Welch, M. G. & Son.............................Burke
Whipple, L. W. & Son..........................Malone
Whitney, C. P.................................Orleans
Will, John...........................Fort Covington
Winter, N. H................................Cortland
Wood, J. Walter, Jr...........................Clayton
Zabriskie, Andrew C.........................Barrytown

NORTH DAKOTA.
Pope, G. Stanley..............................Oacoma

OHIO.
Beatty, J. P................................Pataskala
Betts, Henry ....Pittsfield
Cook, Howard..................................Beloit
Crane, J. H. & Sons............................Toledo
Greenawalt, J. S. & Son........................Beloit

Howatt, D. E.....................................Cleveland
McConnell, A. B. & Son....................Wellington
Spencer, A. B..................................Goldwood
Wilson, A. J....................................Grafton

OREGON.

Honeyman, J. D................................Portland

PENNSYLVANIA.

Ayer, H. S......................................Columbus
Blakeslee, O. P..............................Spartansburg
Boyer, R. A...................................Catasauqua
Butterfield, Jerome F...................South Montrose
Byrne, Christopher........................Friendsville
Byrne, Patrick................................St. Josephs
Carrons, Robert M..........................Washington
Cass, George L..................................Sunbury
Cloud, James & Son....................Kennet Square
Cornell, A. M......................................Altus
Cornell, H. S...................Columbia Cross Roads
Davis, Edward Parker.........................Newton
Farrell, W. E......................................Corry
Friends' Asylum..............Frankford, Philadelphia
Hillview Stock Farm, Limited....................Paoli
Hopkins, Willis W...........................Aldenville
Logan, Sidney A............................Philadelphia
McCray, C. F. & Son..............................Corry
McFadden, George H........................Bryn Mawr
Munce, R. J...................................Washington
Oakey, John W...............................Bryn Mawr
Peck, C. L....................................Coudersport
Roberts, Percival, Jr.........................Narberth
Shimer, A. S....................................Redington
Shimer, B. Luther...............................Bethlehem
Simpson, John..................................Scranton
Stewart, C. E..................................Hartstown
Templeton, Robert & Son........................Ulster

Turnbull, Thomas, Jr......835 Western Ave, Allegheny
Valentine, John R........................Bryn Mawr

RHODE ISLAND.

Angell, Edwin G.........................Providence
Bowen, Edward S.........................Pawtucket
Brown Obadiah, Estate of................Providence
Hawes, Addison S........................Providence
Joslin, H. S..............................Mohegan
Sherman, Everett B......................Harrisville
Sherman, Leander ....Harrisville
Smith, Benjamin F..................North Scituate
Smith, Daniel A............................Tarkiln
Tefft, S. Frank...........................Hamilton
Vaughn, William P......................Providence
Winsor, Nicholas S.......................Greenville

SOUTH CAROLINA.

Clayton, B. F. & Son......................Anderson
Hinson, W. G............................Charleston

SOUTH DAKOTA.

Cosgrove, Michael..........................Madison

TEXAS.

Turner, J. C.............................Long View

VIRGINIA.

Groome, H. C.............................Warrenton
Turnbull, Thomas, Jr.....................Casanova
Venable, A. R., Jr.......................Farmville

VERMONT.

Abell, C. A..............................St. Albans
Anderson, A. J. & Son...............North Craftsbury
Buck, C. W..............................Brownsville
Butterfield, B. F.......................Derby Line
Clark, H. A..............................Hyde Park
Cramton, W. S..............................Rutland

Davidson, George .... Swanton
Drew, F. A................................ South Burlington
Dunsmore, George .... Swanton
Emerson, Charles W......................... Charlotte
Fisher & May.............................. St. Albans Hill
Fletcher, A. M............................ Proctorsville
Forest Park Farm.......................... Brandon
Foss, J. Barron........................... St. Albans
Hannah, Matthew .... Brownsville
Houghton, W. W............................ Lyndonville
Jackman, W. H............................. Vergennes
Joslyn, F. A.............................. Northfield
Lovejoy & Eddy............................ Stowe
Merriam, W. A............................. Glover
Nye, W. C................................. East Barre
Parker, R. & Son.......................... Ferrisburgh
Proctor, Fletcher D....................... Proctor
Rice, George L............................ Rutland
Sanford, Charles .... Ludlow
Scott, W. F............................... Brandon
Scribner, G. S., Estate of................ Castleton
Spalding, L. C. & Son..................... Poultney
Stevens, C. B............................. St. Johnsbury
Stevens, Wm. Stanford..................... St. Albans
Turner, Walter D.......................... Moretown
Vaughan, C. A. & R. H..................... Thetford Centre, Vt.
Vermont Experiment Station................ Burlington
Vermont Industrial School................. Vergennes
Watson, H. R. C........................... Brandon
Winslow, C. M............................. Brandon

WASHINGTON.

Clise, J. W............................... Seattle

WEST VIRGINIA.

Reymann, L. A............................. Wheeling

WISCONSIN.

Finn, James ....Whitewater
Jones, Sam ....Juneau
Seitz, Adam ....Waukesha
Tschudy, Fred ....Monroe

RESIDENCE UNKNOWN.

Birnie, Charles A.
Bradford, A. H.
Crane, Fred
Davidson, George
Fairweather, William
Gibb, J. L.
Haskins, J. P.
Krebs, J. DeWitt
Robinson, Isaac R.
Smith, J. B.
Thurber, C. S.
Walcott, C. W.
Wood, Lucius H.

CANADA.

Cochran, M. H......................Compton, Que.
Clark, J. G..........................Ottawa, Ont.
Hume, Alex & Co......................Menie, Ont.
Hunter, Robert & Sons................Maxville, Ont.
Irving, Thomas ....Petite Cote, Que.
Ness, R. R..........................Howick, Que.
Stephen, W. F....................Huntingdon, Que.

A PAPER

Read Before the Fourth Annual Meeting of the American Breeders' Association at Washington, D. C., January 28th 1908, by C. M. Winslow, Secretary of the Ayrshire Breeders' Association, Brandon, Vermont.

METHODS USED BY THE AYRSHIRE BREEDERS' ASSOCIATION IN PERFECTING THE BREED.

The mention of the name of Scotland always suggests to the mind a country of rugged exterior, of fierce winds and terrific storms; the name of Scotchman, sterling grit and hardy constitution, so when we mention the Ayrshire cow, the suggestion is of an animal fitted for a life of daily battle for sustenance, against all the opposing elements of nature.

The County of Ayr, in which the Ayrshire breed of cattle originated, is situated in the southwest of Scotland, backed by mountains on the east and washed by the ocean on the west, having the form of a crescent and embracing the Firth of Clyde in its circle. The face of the country is hilly, and rises from the level of the sea some 2,000 feet to the top of the mountains on the east. The soil is strong and somewhat heavy, being a clay and clay-loam, but thinner on the tops of the hills and mountains, the whole being originally covered with a dense growth of timber. The climate is moist, with a temperature ranging from about twenty-five to sixty-five degrees, with a mean temperature of about forty-seven degrees, regulated by its proximity to the sea, and with frequent rains, which are favorable to growth of grass, giving luxuriant pasturage, though sometimes the country is swept by fierce coast storms.

The Ayrshire is probably the youngest of the thoroughbred dairy breeds, and though her origin is veiled in some obscurity there are many things that confirm the theory that the native wild cattle of the country are the foundation of the Ayrshire of modern times. The original native wild cattle of the country were said to be white, with red ears and black noses, high white horns with black tips, with an animal now and then having more of the brown, black or red, very wild, and the bulls fierce, but when calves are taken young grow to be quiet and tame. This theory seems the more reasonable when we consider how easily the Ayrshire color reverts to the white; then too there is frequently an Ayrshire that has a strong tendency to that wild, alert bearing that characterized the foundation stock.

The first we hear of any effort being made to improve the native stock of the country was about the year 1700, and this was said to have been accomplished by selection and better care.

We read from Aiton that about 1750 the Earl of Marchmont purchased from the Bishop of Durham, and carried to his seat in Berwickshire, several cows and a bull of the Teeswater or other English breed, of a brown and white color. He also writes that about 1770, bulls and cows of the Teeswater or Shorthorn breed were said to have been introduced by several proprietors, and it is from them and their crosses with the native stock that the present dairy breed has been formed.

In 1811, in "Survey of Ayrshire," Aiton writes that the Ayrshire dairy breed is "in a great measure the native indigenous breed of the County of Ayr, improved in their size, shapes and qualities, chiefly by judicious selection, cross coupling, feeding and treatment for a long series of time and with much judgment and attention.

From about the beginning of the last century we find frequent mention of efforts for improvement in the shape of body, and especially in the shape of the udder.

Ayrshires were very early brought into Canada by the Scotch settlers, also were brought over on ships from Glasgow to supply milk during the voyage, and were sold on arrival at Montreal or Quebec, and so popular were these cows that shipmasters were commissioned to bring over one or more cows from Ayrshire. More recently Ayrshires have been imported into Canada in large numbers. The importation to the United States began about 1837, by the Massachusetts Society for Promotion of Agriculture bringing a few head into the state and scattering them among the farmers of Massachusetts. Other importations from Scotland followed at intervals into different parts of the United States, as the value of this breed for dairy purposes was made evident, and as the demand became greater than the home breeders could supply.

The Ayrshire cow in general is a handsome, sprightly looking cow of medium size, weighing at maturity about 1,000 pounds, red and white in color, the relative proportions of red and white being greatly varied and readily yielding to the taste of the breeder, from his skill in selecting breeding animals.

There has of late seemed to be more inquiry for Ayrshires with white preponderating, but color is merely a matter of fancy and carries with it no excellence of dairy quality.

The Ayrshire has a small, bony head, large, full eyes, dish face, broad muzzle, large mouth, upright horns, the size, whether slim or large, being a matter of local taste in breeding, long, slim neck, clean cut at throat, thin, sloping shoulders, with the spine rising a little above the shoulder blades, back level to setting on of tail, except a rise at the pelvic arch, broad across the loin, barrel deep and large, with ribs well sprung to give abundant room for storing coarse fodder, and wide through the region of the heart and lungs. Hips wide apart, rump long, hind legs straight, thighs thin and incurving, giving room for udder, legs short, bones small, joints firm, udder large and square, and on young cows it is nearly level with belly, wide, long and strongly hung, teats from two and a half to three and a half inches long, of good size, placed wide apart on the four corners of the udder, with udder level between the teats and not cut up, milk veins large and tortuous, entering the belly well forward towards the fore legs. Skin soft and mellow, covered with a thick growth of fine hair.

While an Ayrshire cow should be shapely and handsome to look at as she stands or walks, she should when handled reveal much looseness of vertebra, flatness of rib, and width between the ribs indicating large dairy capacity. The Ayrshire is a tough, hardy cow, with a vigorous appetite, and not too particular what she eats. She is always hungry, eats greedily and chews her cud rapidly. You can rarely see an Ayrshire cow when not either taking in food or chewing what she has already gathered. While at pasture she does not wander around looking for sweet patches of grass, but goes to work rapidly gathering what is most convenient, either of grass or browse, and when full lies down to chew her cud with no time wasted; and when going to and from pasture will chew her cud while walking, and often continues to chew when started into a run.

The general appearance of an Ayrshire, as you look at her, is striking, being alert and full of life and reserved energy. She is a healthy cow, rarely having ailments of body or udder, and you seldom see an Ayrshire cow but that has four healthy quarters in her udder and gives a uniform quantity of milk from each. She is a very persistent milker, giving a uniform quantity well up towards calving, and many of them are dried off with difficulty.

She is very intelligent, quick to learn and of a retentive memory, easily taught to take the same place in the stable and, if required to change, will in a few days readily take the new place. She is quiet and pleasant to milk, not easily disturbed, and will as a rule yield her milk as readily to one milker as to another, and does not seem disturbed by any amount of noise in the stable.

As a dairy cow she is particularly adapted to the production of milk for the milkman and for table use, as her medium size, vigorous appetite and easy keeping qualities make her an economical producer, while her even, uniform production makes her a reliable supply, and the richness of her milk in total solids places it above suspicion from city milk inspectors. Her milk is particularly adapted to transportation, as it does not churn or sour easily, and when poured back and forth a few times will readily mix the cream back into the milk, which will not again readily separate, giving it a uniform quality until the last is sold or used. It has a good body, is rich looking and never looks blue. The milk itself being evenly balanced with casein and butter fat is a complete food, easily digested, nutritious, and is particularly adapted to children and invalids. Stomachs that are weak and unable to digest other milk, find no trouble with Ayrshire cow's milk.

Until recently, in Scotland, Canada and the United States, the effort of breeders of Ayrshire cattle has been directed towards a uniformly high standard of dairy production from the breed as a whole, little attention being paid to developing the individual superiority of the breed in her dairy yield. This quality of the Ayrshire, the result of the general breeding, was particularly noticeable at the Pan American Exhibition in the comparative dairy yield of the Ayrshire with that of other dairy breeds. That test showed the least margin of difference between the highest and lowest dairy yield in the Ayrshire of any of the breeds, showing a uniformly high class of cows, none phenomenally good and none particularly poor, but with remarkably uniform yields.

Of late years the Scotch have instituted a form of test for two days, called the Derby, testing the cow in the ring as a show cow, and again at home as a dairy cow, combining the two in making the final award.

In Canada the Canadian government has recently instituted periodical tests of different dairy breeds under the specific direction of each breed through its Association, the expense of which is paid for by the Canadian government.

Under this management the Canadian Ayrshire Association have recently formulated rules and regulations for governing a series of yearly tests for Ayrshire cows to admit them to advanced registry. This will gradually bring to the front the best specimens of the breed for dairy production, and will give an opportunity for progressive breeders to bring into their lines of breeding an advancement of dairy production.

In the United States there have been a few breeders who for a good many years kept private records of the amount of milk given by the individual cows in their herds, but until the advent of the Babcock tester there was no uniform method by which the breeder could know the quality of the milk, consequently only one side of the yield from his cows was known. Since the Experiment Stations throughout the United States have, in their experimental work, turned their attention to the skillful handling of the milk, the Ayrshire Breeders' Association have established a system of Home Dairy Tests for the breed, carefully guarded at home against mistakes, and periodically inspected by the Experiment Station where the herd is located. At the last annual meeting the Association, in order to doubly guard the work done in testing, changed the rules governing the tests, adopted monthly inspection by the Experiment Stations and dropped all but yearly tests.

It is the belief of the Ayrshire Breeders' Association that while daily, weekly and monthly tests are interesting, in a way, they are misleading as to the real value of a cow, and the desire of the Association is to produce and make public the real profit derived from the cow in her normal condition, doing her regular dairy work of a breeding and dairy cow. A cow must be kept the whole year at an expense, and whether or not she is a paying investment depends upon the receipts from her for the full time she is kept. She might be forced to a phenomenal yield for a week or a month, which if taken as the guide for the whole year would make her a very profitable cow, when, in reality, the short yields were no guide at all for the whole time, and no index as to the dairy profit received from the cow.

It is, perhaps, too soon to predict the the future of the youngest of the dairy breeds, but the few results we have obtained from official tests since the system was inaugurated, have raised high hopes for the future standing of this breed in the production of dairy products of a high order with a minimum cost for production.

The show ring being the medium of presenting the breed to the public for observation, has always attracted the attention of the general public, for the efforts of breeders and the scale of points all coincide in producing a very handsome and attractive cow, but whether she will retain her shapeliness when generations of utility have forced her dairy productiveness to the point which it now looks as though she would soon occupy, is a question that can be answered only in time.

The dairy future of the Ayrshire cow is assured, and a position of no mean order awaits her in the supply of the dairy product for the milk trade, and also in the production of butter; but to obtain a leadership in utility she must sacrifice some of the beauty lines that have for so long attracted the eye of the beholder. It has been thought by some breeders that the Ayrshire cow might be bred for both the show ring and the dairy, which is true when style and beauty, with an abundant supply of dairy yield, is the end sought; but when the fullest capacity of the Ayrshire cow as a dairy cow is obtained, either public opinion as to the highest type in the Ayrshire cow must undergo a change or there will be a double standard of appreciation, the cow that wears the ribbons in public, and the cow that earns the money at home.

While it is for too short a time that the Association has been testing Ayrshire cows to form a general opinion as to their uniform yield in dairy products, still we have enough official yields reported to give an inspiring hope for the future when breeders shall, with the same system in selection that has been the means of advancement in other breeds, select their breeding stock from producing families, that have come to the front in the Association Home Dairy tests, and Advanced Registry tests. The result of such a course would naturally tend to place the Ayrshire cow of the United States and Canada in the dairy producing class and the Ayrshire of Scotland in the show ring class, until such time as the public comes to see beauty lines in utility conformation, or until such time as the breeders of Scotland fall into line with Canada and the States in pushing the Ayrshire cow to the front as a dairy producer. The time during which the Ayrshire Breeders' Association has been conducting official tests of individual Ayrshire cows is so short, and the cows so few that have been tested, that any data we might present to the public would be simply indicative of their dairy ability, and not conclusive evidence. With some hesitation we submit the following as being complete results to date of the tests for advanced registry, trusting that this is but a forerunner of greater numbers, and an earnest of better things in the future, when the whole of the breeders of Ayrshire cattle shall awake to the importance of official tests in giving information as to the individual value of their breeding herds. The retaining of the best as breeders, and the elimination of the poorest from the herd, from knowledge derived from the official tests for dairy excellence, would in a short time place the Ayrshire cow as an economical producer of high class dairy products, in a position where she would hold a high position in all dairy sections, and especially where the natural conditions were adverse to successful dairying.

We have admitted 120 cows and heifers to advanced registry since we began, divided as to age as follows:

Four heifers, under two years old at time of beginning the test, gave for 365 consecutive days from beginning the test an average of 7,091 lbs. of milk and 335 lbs. of butter.

Thirty-nine two-year-olds gave an average of 7,127 lbs. of milk and 329 lbs. of butter.

Sixteen three-year-olds gave an average of 8,281 lbs. of milk and 387 lbs. of butter.

Ten four-year-olds gave an average of 9,463 lbs. of milk and 431 lbs. of butter.

Fifty-one mature cows gave an average of 9,672 lbs. of milk and 436 lbs. of butter.

The following are some of the individual records in the different ages:

UNDER TWO YEARS OLD.

Bonnie 2d of Radnor 19754, bred by Geo. H. McFadden, Bryn Mawr, Pa., owned and tested by J. W. Clise, Seattle, Wash., gave 8,184 lbs. of milk and 403 lbs. of butter.

Lilac of Radnor 18690, bred, owned and tested by Geo. H. McFadden, Bryn Mawr, Pa., gave 7,778 lbs. of milk and 351 lbs. of butter.

TWO YEAR OLD FORM.

Baby Douglas 21849, bred, owned and tested by L. A. Reymann, Wheeling, W. Va., gave 9,654 lbs. of milk and 440 lbs. of butter.

Letta Lind of Radnor 17892, bred, owned and tested by Geo. H. McFadden, Bryn Mawr, Pa., gave 8,602 lbs. of milk and 435 lbs. of butter.

THREE YEAR OLD FORM.

Sweet Josie 19833, bred by J. D. Honeyman, Portland, Oregon, owned and tested by J. W. Clise, Seattle, Wash., gave 10,103 lbs. of milk and 472 lbs. of butter.

Babe's Duchess 22213, bred, owned and tested by L. A. Reymann, Wheeling, W. Va., gave 9,559 lbs. milk and 452 lbs. of butter.

Eugenie Douglas 17452, bred, owned and tested by Howard Cook, Beloit, O., gave 9,587 lbs. of milk and 443 lbs. of butter.

Lady Bell 4th 17256, bred, owned and tested by John R. Valentine, Bryn Mawr, Pa., gave 8,516 lbs. of milk and 437 lbs. of butter.

FOUR YEAR OLD FORM.

Finlayston Maggie 3d 19217, imported, owned and tested by Geo. H. McFadden, Bryn Mawr, Pa., gave 10,759 lbs. of milk and 513 lbs. of butter.

Becky of Holehouse 17015, imported, owned and tested by Geo. H. McFadden, Bryn Mawr, Pa., gave 10,507 lbs. of milk and 463 lbs. of butter.

Madonna Lass 2d 17473, bred, owned and tested by L. A. Reymann, Wheeling, W. Va., gave 10,020 lbs. of milk and 449 lbs. of butter.

MATURE COWS.

Polly Puss 16296, bred by W. G. Tucker, Elm Valley, N. Y., owned and tested by John R. Valentine, Bryn Mawr, Pa., gave 12,632 lbs. of milk and 584 lbs. of butter.

Rena Myrtle 9530, bred by C. M. Winslow, Brandon, Vt., owned and tested by the Vermont Experiment Station, Burlington, Vt., gave 12,172 lbs. of milk and 546 lbs. of butter.

Denty 9th of Auchenbrain 15577, imported, owned and tested by Geo. H. McFadden, Bryn Mawr, Pa., gave 11,757 lbs. of milk and 528 lbs. of butter.

Miss Ollie 12039, bred, owned and tested by L. S. Drew, South Burlington, Vt., gave 9,924 lbs. of milk and 514 lbs. of butter.

Keepsake 15913, bred by W. G. Tucker, Elm Valley, N. Y., owned and tested by John R. Valentine, Bryn Mawr, Pa., gave 10,868 lbs. of milk and 513 lbs. of butter.

Rena Ross 14539, bred by W. G. Tucker, Elm Valley, N. Y., owned and tested by John R. Valentine, Bryn Mawr, Pa., gave 10,065 lbs. of milk and 512 lbs. of butter.

Kitty K. 12933, bred by W. G. Tucker, Elm Valley, N. Y., owned and tested by John R. Valentine, Bryn Mawr, Pa., gave 11,115 lbs. of milk and 512 lbs. of butter.

Durwood 12680, bred by Charles H. Hayes & Son,

Portsmouth, N. H., owned and tested by E. J. Fletcher, Greenfield, N. H., gave 10,701 lbs. of milk and 506 lbs. of butter.

Acelista 12094, bred, owned and tested by C. M. Winslow, Brandon, Vt., gave for five consecutive years an official test of 52,000 lbs. of milk and 2,137 lbs. of butter, and dropped five calves.

Three full sisters, Durwood, Durline and Durtharlynne, bred by Charles H. Hayes & Son, Portsmouth, N. H., gave by official test 30,363 lbs. of milk and 1,347 lbs. of butter in a year, or an average of 10,121 lbs. of milk and 449 lbs. of butter.

The Ayrshire Record.

ADVANCED REGISTRY.

VOLUME II.

BULLS.

6180 Duke of Ayer 4 (2d entry).

Calved December 29, 1896, bred by W. G. Tucker, Elm Valley, N. Y., owned by W. V. Probasco, Cream Ridge, N. J.

Dam Kalley 12660; sire Major Ayer 5533.

Sire of two in Volume 1 and two in Volume 2 Advanced Register.

6248 Glencairn of Ridgeside 5.

Calved July 27, 1896, bred by Robert Reford, Ste. Anne de Bellevue, Que., owned by S. M. Wells, Wethersfield, Conn.

Dam White Floss 13343; sire Glencairn 3d 6247.

Sire of two in the Advanced Register.

7312 Nox'emall 6.

Calved April 10, 1899, bred by J. F. Converse, Woodville, N. Y., owned by L. A. Reymann, Wheeling, West Virginia.

Dam Viola Drummond 12533; sire Lord Douglas I of Maple Grove 6376.

Sire of four in the Advanced Register.

8228 Moonstone of Drumsuie 7.

Calved April, 1900, bred by William Winter, Scotland, owned by George H. McFadden, Bryn Mawr, Pa.

Dam Browny 2d of Drumsuie "13386"; sire Lord Percy of Drumsuie "4427."

Sire of four in the Advanced Register.

6634 Carbello 8.

Calved June 22, 1900, bred and owned by C. M. Winslow & Son, Brandon, Vt.

Dam Rose Sultana 12072; sire Reynard 6038.

Sire of three in the Advanced Register.

7670 Geo. of Rosemont 9.

Calved February 28, 1900, bred by Robert M. Reid, Scotland, owned by Geo. H. McFadden, Bryn Mawr, Pa.

Dam Flora 3d of Bonshaw 15575; sire Shamrock of Bonshaw "4200."

Sire of six in the Advanced Register.

6044 Rothage 10.

Calved August 4, 1898, bred and owned by C. M. Winslow & Son, Brandon, Vt.

Dam Clio Rose 7525; sire Goldrick 5345.

Sire of two in the Advanced Register.

7225 Oshawa of Highland 11.

Calved June 23, 1898, bred by the Estate of Thomas Guy, Oshawa, Ont., owned by John R. Valentine, Bryn Mawr, Pa.

Dam Oshawa Lass 6th 14238; sire Eva's Heir 7197.

Sire of three in the Advanced Register.

5651 Twister 12.

Calved August 14, 1896, bred by C. M. Winslow & Son, Brandon, Vt., owned by L. A. Reymann, Wheeling, West Virginia.

Dam Rose Allie 11154; sire Nonpareil 4535.

Sire of three in the Advanced Register.

5533 Major Ayer 13.

Calved July 16, 1893, bred by Alonzo Libby, Westbrook, Maine, owned by W. G. Tucker, Elm Valley, N. Y.

Dam Queen Sadie 7534; sire George A. F. 4227.

Sire of seven in the Advanced Register.

7168 Colonel Ayer 14.

Calved April 29, 1900, bred by W. G. Tucker, Elm Valley, N. Y., owned by John R. Valentine, Bryn Mawr, Pa.

Dam Pink Hebron 12907; sire Major Ayer 5533.

Sire of six in the Advanced Register.

6711 Prince of Barclay 15.

Calved June 19, 1898, bred and owned by George H. McFadden, Bryn Mawr, Pa.

Dam Snowflake of Burnhouses 15088; sire Royalty of Monkland 6704.

Sire of five in the Advanced Register.

6705 Tam Oshanta 16.

Calved March, 1896, bred and owned by George H. McFadden, Bryn Mawr, Pa.

Dam Snowflake of Burnhouses 15088; sire Royalty of Monkland 6704.

Sire of two in the Advanced Register.

6775 Beloit Ayer 17.

Calved October, 25, 1898, bred by W. G. Tucker, Elm Valley, N. Y., owned by Howard Cook, Beloit, Ohio.

Dam Pearl Clyde 13991; sire Major Ayer 5533.

Sire of two in the Advanced Register.

4692 Calmar 18.

Calved August 14, 1890, bred by C. M. Winslow & Son, Brandon, Vt., owned by George H. Yeaton, Dover, N. H.

Dam Doxy 4400; sire Casino 3900.

Sire of two in the Advanced Register.

COWS.

Seven day tests.

21597 Lucretia B. of Riverside 32.

Calved September 8, 1903, bred by O. P. Blakeslee, Spartansburg, Pa., owned by J. F. Converse, Woodville, New York.

Dam Lucretia B 11630, sire Glencairn of Menie 6829.

Home Dairy Test June 7, 1906, to June 14, 1906; two years and 271 day old at beginning the test.

Record 227 lbs. of milk and 10 lbs. of butter.

22741 Beauty B. 33.

Calved September 8, 1904, bred by O. P. Blakeslee, Spartansburg, Pa., owned by J. F. Converse, Woodville, New York.

Dam Nettie B. 22739; sire Glencairn of Menie 6829.
Home Dairy Test July 12, 1907, to July 18 inclusive.
Two years and 323 days old at beginning of test.
Record 248 lbs. of milk and 11 lbs. of butter.

13449 Roseleaf Douglas 34.
Calved August 10, 1896, bred and owned by J. F. Converse, Woodville, N. Y.
Dam Gert Douglas 11813; sire Carlton Victor 5276.
Home Dairy Test. Mature.
Record 357 lbs. of milk and 15 lbs. of butter.

9670 Annie Bert 35.
Calved January 3, 1887, bred by W. R. Garvin, Dover, N. H., owned by George H. Yeaton, Dover, N. H.
Dam Rosie Wyber 9352; sire Roldan 4259.
New Hampshire Experiment Station Test. Mature.
Record 356 lbs. of milk and 145 lbs. of butter.

11882 Ouija 36.
Calved May 23, 1892, bred and owned by George H. Yeaton, Dover, N. H.
Dam Jeannette Guelph 9673; sire Jasper 4841.
New Hampshire Experiment Station Test. Mature.
Record 377.7 lbs. of milk and 15.4 lbs. of butter.

20951 Kirkland Sparrow 37.
Calved March, 1900, bred by G. B. Meikle, Scotland, owned by Percival Roberts, Jr., Narberth, Pa.
Dam Kirkland Stonechat "18336"; sire Tower Peter "5065."
Home Dairy Test, August, 1907. Mature.
Record 382.2 lbs of milk and 17.77 lbs. of butter.

365 Day Test of Heifers in Their Two-year-old Form in Order of Age.

18695 May Rose of Radnor 38.

Calved October 24, 1903, bred and owned by Geo. H. McFadden, Bryn Mawr, Pa.

Dam Lady Burnhouses 15092; sire Moonstone of Drumsuie 8228, imported.

Home Dairy Test 1905-6. One year and 297 days old at beginning of test.

Record 6,898 lbs. of milk and 336 lbs. of butter.

17512 Florine Corslet 39.

Calved February 11, 1902, bred and owned by C. M. Winslow & Son, Brandon, Vt.

Dam Floy Corslet 15023; sire Warfield 7045.

Home Dairy Test 1904-5. One year and 325 days old at beginning of test.

Record 5,504 lbs. of milk and 248 lbs. of butter.

19754 Bonnie 2d of Radnor 40.

Calved August 13, 1904, bred and owned by Geo. H. McFadden, Bryn Mawr, Pa.

Dam Bonnie of Radnor 17012, imp.; sire Moonstone of Drumsuie 8228, imp.

Home Dairy Test 1906-7. One year and 352 days old at beginning of test.

Record 8,184 lbs. of milk and 403 lbs. of butter.

18264 Muriel Girl 41.

Calved October 22, 1903, bred and owned by C. M. Winslow & Son, Brandon, Vt.

Dam Muriel Fox 15036; sire Carbello 6634.

Home Dairy Test 1905-6. One year and 359 days old at beginning of test.

Record 5,914 lbs. of milk and 285 lbs. of butter.

18690 Lilac of Radnor 42.

Calved July 29, 1903, bred and owned by Geo. H. McFadden, Bryn Mawr, Pa.

Dam Fancy of Auchenbrain 16834; sire Geo. of Rosemont 7670, imp.

Home Dairy Test 1905-6. One year and 360 days old at beginning of test.

Record 7,778 lbs. of milk and 351 lbs. of butter.

17904 Bessie of Rosemont 43.

Calved February 15, 1903, bred and owned by Geo. H. McFadden, Bryn Mawr, Pa.

Dam Mayflower of Monkland 15090; sire Moonstone of Drumsuie 8228, imp.

Home Dairy Test 1905-6. Two years and 20 days old at beginning of test.

Record 8,835 lbs. of milk and 433 lbs. of butter.

17507 Rose Crashaw 44.

Calved August 17, 1901, bred and owned by C. M. Winslow & Son, Brandon, Vt.

Dam Rose Caprice 13681; sire Rothage 6044.

Home Dairy Test 1903-4. Two years and 25 days old at beginning of test.

Record 5,995 lbs. of milk and 269 lbs. of butter.

19753 Ruth 2d of Barclay 45.

Calved June 14, 1904, bred and owned by Geo. H McFadden, Bryn Mawr, Pa.

Dam Ruth of Barclay 17023; sire Geo. of Rosemont 7670, imp.

Home Dairy Test 1906-7. Two years and 26 days old at beginning of test.

Record 6,338 lbs. of milk and 340 lbs. of butter.

18256 Sibyl Corslet 46.

Calved October 19, 1902, bred and owned by C. M. Winslow & Son, Brandon, Vt.

Dam Alfreda Corslet 15018; sire Carbello 6634.

Home Dairy Test 1904-5. Two years and 34 days old at beginning of test.

Record 7,170 lbs. of milk and 317 lbs. of butter.

18043 Lady Wonder 4th 47.

Calved October 1, 1902, bred and owned by L. S. Drew, South Burlington, Vt.

Dam Lady Wonder 14158; sire Starlight 7075.

Home Dairy Test 1904-5. Two years and 35 days old at beginning of test.

Record 5,606 lbs. of milk and 245 lbs. of butter.

19615 Myrtle K. 48.

Calved July 15, 1903, bred and owned by Walter D. Turner, Moretown, Vt.

Dam Dollie Kilbowie 16779; sire Ashmont 7542.

Home Dairy Test 1905-6. Two years and 63 days old at beginning of test.

Record 7,497 lbs. of milk and 293 lbs. of butter.

20366 Isabella of Sand Hill 49.

Calved October 1, 1904, bred and owned by S. S. Karr & Sons, Almond, N. Y.

Dam Irene Park 18362; sire Earl's Choice of Spring Hill 8289.

Home Dairy Test 1906-7. Two years and 85 days old at beginning of test.

Record 7,887 lbs. of milk and 373 lbs. of butter.

18255 Rose Aileen 50.

Calved September 13, 1902, bred and owned by C. M. Winslow & Son, Brandon, Vt.

Dam Rose Erica 12775; sire Carbello 6634.

Home Dairy Test 1904-5. Two years and 86 days old at beginning of test.

Record 6,256 lbs. of milk and 248 lbs. of butter.

20365 Bessie of Sand Hill 51.

Calved September 11, 1904, bred and owned by S. S. Karr & Sons, Almond, N. Y.

Dam Miss Betty of Spring Hill 17997; sire Prince of Sand Hill 8479.

Home Dairy Test 1906-7. Two years and 105 days old at beginning of test.

Record 7,307 lbs. of milk and 376 lbs. of butter.

17511 Rose Claymore 52.

Calved December 30, 1901, bred and owned by C. M. Winslow & Son, Brandon, Vt.

Dam Rose Clockston 15026; sire Rothage 6044.

Home Dairy Test 1904-5. Two years and 110 days old at beginning of test.

Record 6,542 lbs. of milk and 314 lbs. of butter.

17453 Pearl Douglas 53.

Calved April 7, 1901, bred and owned by Howard Cook, Beloit, Ohio.

Dam Little Douglas 12769; sire Beloit Ayer 6775.

Home Dairy Test 1903-4. Two years and 116 days old at beginning of test.

Record 6,598 lbs. of milk and 317 lbs. of butter.

17900 Buttercup of Rosemont 54.

Calved July 1, 1902, bred and owned by George H. McFadden, Bryn Mawr, Pa.

Dam Lady Stair of Holehouse 15574, imp.; sire Dewey Auchenbrain 6708, imp.

Home Dairy Test 1904-5. Two years and 122 days old at beginning of test.

Record 7,584 lbs. of milk and 356 lbs. of butter.

20180 Bell Ayer 55.

Calved October 13, 1903, bred and owned by John R. Valentine, Bryn Mawr, Pa.

Dam Lady Bell 3d 17253; sire Colonel Ayer 7168.

Home Dairy Test 1906-7. Two years and 126 days old at beginning of test.

Record 7,111 lbs. of milk and 361 lbs. of butter.

18687 Francis of Barclay 56.

Calved March 18, 1903, bred and owned by George H. McFadden, Bryn Mawr, Pa.

Dam Queen of Barclay 15096; sire Moonstone of Drumsuie 8228, imp.

Home Dairy Test 1905-6. Two years and 128 days old at beginning of test.

Record 8,047 lbs. of milk and 403 lbs. of butter.

19748 Queen 2d of Barclay 57.

Calved March 18, 1904, bred by George H. McFadden, Bryn Mawr, Pa., owned by J. W. Clise, Redmond, Washington.

Dam Queen of Barclay 15096, imp.; sire Geo. of Rosemont 7670, imp.

Home Dairy Test 1906-7. Two years and 136 days old at beginning of test.

Record 9,486 lbs. of milk and 425 lbs. of butter.

22472 Grace of Sand Hill 58.

Calved September 5, 1904, bred by Hiram Karr, Almond, N. Y., owned by S. S. Karr & Sons, Almond, N. Y.

Dam Viola of Sand Hill 22470; sire Earl's Choice of Spring Hill 8289.

Home Dairy Test 1907-8. Two years and 136 days old at beginning of test.

Record 8,698 lbs. of milk and 395 lbs. of butter.

18262 Myrtle Kilbowie 59.

Calved July 28, 1903, bred by Oliver Smith & Son, Chateaugay, N. Y., owned by C. M. Winslow & Son, Brandon, Vt.

Dam Myrtle Beppo 15396; sire Essex Boy 6904.

Home Dairy Test 1905-6. Two years and 145 days old at beginning of test.

Record 7,199 lbs. of milk and 328 lbs. of butter.

21109 Crimson Rambler 60.

Calved March 28, 1904, bred and owned by George F. Stone, Littleton, Mass.

Dam Crimsonia 2d 13715; sire Duke of Littleton 8080.

Home Dairy Test 1906-7. Two years and 146 days old at beginning of test.

Record 7,988 lbs. of milk and 325 lbs. of butter.

19746 Mosshawk of Barclay 61.

Calved February 21, 1904, bred by George H. McFadden, Bryn Mawr, Pa., owned by J. W. Clise, Redmond, Washington.

Dam Mosshawk of Hindsward 15095, imp.; sire Geo. of Rosemont 7670, imp.

Home Dairy Test 1906-7. Two years and 160 days old at beginning of test.

Record 6,086 lbs. of milk and 299 lbs. of butter.

17431 Felicia of Woodview 62.

Calved November 4, 1900, bred and owned by W. V. Probasco, Cream Ridge, N. J.

Dam Pearl Clyde 13991; sire Duke of Ayer 6180.

Home Dairy Test 1903-4. Two years and 169 days old at beginning of test.

Record 7,048 lbs. of milk and 326 lbs. of butter.

19936 Ruby Russell 3d 63.

Calved June 9, 1904, bred and owned by Henry Dorrance, Plainfield, Conn.

Dam Ruby Russell 15564; sire Judge Mitchell 7502.

Home Dairy Test 1906-7. Two years and 197 days old at beginning of test.

Record 6,760 lbs. of milk and 285 lbs. of butter.

17094 Dolly Fryer 2d 64.

Calved May 20, 1901, bred and owned by Henry Dorrance, Plainfield, Conn.

Dam Dolly Fryer 13012; sire Benedict Arnold 7240.

Home Dairy Test 1904-5. Two years and 228 days old at beginning of test.

Record 6,485 lbs. of milk and 299 lbs. of butter.

21246 Kitty K 3d 65.

Calved February 2, 1904, bred and owned by John R. Valentine, Bryn Mawr, Pa.

Dam Kitty K 12933; sire Colonel Ayer 7168.

Home Dairy Test 1906-7. Two years and 242 days old at beginning of test.

Record 7,364 lbs. of milk and 384 lbs of butter.

17893 Clotilde of Rosemont 66.

Calved February 13, 1902, bred and owned by George H. McFadden, Bryn Mawr, Pa.

Dam Flora 3d of Bonshaw 15575, imp.; sire Prince of Barclay 6711.

Home Dairy Test 1904-5. Two years and 255 days old at beginning of test.

Record 8,548 lbs. milk and 376 lbs. butter.

21849 Baby Douglas 67.

Calved December 30, 1903, bred and owned by L. A. Reymann, Wheeling, W. Va.

Dam Baby Jewess 14868; sire Nox'emall 7312.

Home Dairy Test 1906-7. Two years and 260 days old at beginning of test.

Record 9,652 lbs. of milk and 440 lbs. of butter.

21247 Rena Ayer 68.

Calved March 2, 1904, bred and owned by John R. Valentine, Bryn Mawr, Pa.

Dam Rena Webb 12479; sire Colonel Ayer 7168.

Home Dairy Test 1906-7; two years and 263 days old at beginning of test.

Record 6,929 lbs. of milk and 357 lbs. of butter.

18696 Snowflight of Radnor 69.

Calved November 1, 1903, bred and owned by George H. McFadden, Bryn Mawr, Pa.

Dam Jessie of Mosshawk 17025; sire Geo. of Rosemont 7670.

Home Dairy Test 1906-7; two years and 264 days old at beginning of test.

Record 8,505 lbs. of milk and 406 lbs. of butter.

20179 Oshawa Lass of Highland 2d 70.

Calved May 23, 1903, bred and owned by John R. Valentine, Bryn Mawr, Pa.

Dam Oshawa Lass of Highland 16534; sire Colonel Ayer 7168.

Home Dairy Test 1906-7; two years and 278 days old at beginning of test.

Record 6,281 lbs. of milk and 307 lbs. of butter.

17432 Megsy Tipperlin 71.

Calved March 19, 1901, bred and owned by W. V. Probasco, Cream Ridge, N. J.

Dam Roma 14197; sire Duke of Ayer 6180.

Home Dairy Test 1903-4; two years and 288 days old at beginning of test.

Record 7,117 lbs. of milk and 315 lbs. of butter.

18249 Oshawa Lady 2d 72.

Calved May 7, 1903, bred and owned by John R. Valentine, Bryn Mawr, Pa.

Dam Oshawa Lady 16020; sire Colonel Ayer 7168.

Home Dairy Test 1906-7; two years and 294 days old at beginning of test.

Record 7,074 lbs. of milk and 356 lbs. of butter.

20511 Rose Eaton 73.

Calved November 5, 1902, bred by William Stanford Stevens, St. Albans, Vt., owned by C. M. Winslow & Son, Brandon, Vt.

Dam Rose Elwin 12080; sire Castleton 6886.

Home Dairy Test 1905-6; two years and 329 days old at beginning of test.

Record 7,783 lbs. of milk and 324 lbs. of butter.

17892 Letta Lind of Radnor 74.

Calved December 13, 1901, bred and owned by George H. McFadden, Bryn Mawr, Pa.

Dam Cherry of Bonshaw 15582, imp.; sire Prince of Barclay 6711.

Home Dairy Test 1904-5; two years and 337 days old at beginning of test.

Record 8,602 lbs. of milk and 435 lbs. of butter.

THREE YEAR OLD FORM.

18821 Lady Rotha 75.

Calved June 18, 1903, bred by S. M. Wells, Newington, Conn., owned by J. W. Clise, Redmond, Washington.

Dam Rotha 12460; sire Glencairn of Ridgeside 6248.

Home Dairy Test 1906-7; three years and 9 days old at beginning of test.

Record 8,101 lbs. of milk and 368 lbs. of butter

17452 Eugenie Douglas 76.

Calved October 10, 1900, bred and owned by Howard Cook, Beloit, Ohio.

Dam Miss Douglas 10265; sire Beloit Ayer 6775.

Home Dairy Test 1903-4; three years and 10 days old at beginning of test.

Record 9,587 lbs. of milk and 443 lbs. of butter.

18689 White Bess of Radnor 77.

Calved July 12, 1903, bred and owned by George H. McFadden, Bryn Mawr, Pa.

Dam Daisy of Rosemont 17011, imp.; sire Geo. of Rosemont 7670 imp.

Home Dairy Test 1906-7; three years and 20 days old at beginning of test.

Record 6,594 lbs of milk and 306 lbs. of butter.

18824 Orinda 78.

Calved July 8, 1903, bred by S. M. Wells, Newington, Conn., owned by J. W. Clise, Redmond, Washington.

Dam Dolly Roy 12462; sire Glencairn of Ridgeside 6248.

Home Dairy Test 1906-7; three years and 23 days old at beginning of test.

Record 7,375 lbs. of milk and 327 lbs. of butter.

16701 Stilletto 79.

Calved September 10, 1900, bred and owned by Connecticut Agricultural College, Storrs, Conn.

Dam Stella Bertram 2d 13432; sire Rudolph 5825.

Connnecticut Experiment Station 1903-4; three years and 42 days old at beginning of test.

Record 6,707 lbs. of milk and 307 lbs. of butter.

17614 Ponemah 2d 80.

Calved August 20, 1902, bred by George H. Yeaton, Dover, N. H., owned by Walter D. Turner, Moretown, Vt.

Home Dairy Test 1905-6; three years and 51 days old at beginning of test.

Record 7,330 lbs. of milk and 301 lbs. of butter.

18248 Neidpath Lassie 2d 81.

Calved March 25 , 1903, bred and owned by John R. Valentine, Bryn Mawr, Pa.

Dam Neidpath Lassie 17260; sire Colonel Ayer 7168.

Home Dairy Test 1906-7; three years and 67 days old at beginning of test.

Record 6,746 lbs of milk and 301 lbs. of butter.

19487 Midget of Sand Hill 82.

Calved September 8, 1903, bred by M. J. & I. D. Karr, Almond, N. Y., owned by S. S. Karr & Sons, Almond. New York.

Dam Kathleen T. 13286; sire John Doland 7872.

Home Dairy Test 1906-7; three years and 108 days old at beginning of test.

Record 9,824 lbs. of milk and 422 lbs. of butter.

19489 Cora T 3d 83.

Calved November 8, 1903, bred and owned by S. S. Karr & Sons, Almond, N. Y.

Dam Cora T 13772; sire John Doland 7872.

Home Dairy Test 1907-8; three years and 118 days old at beginning of test.

Record 7,312 lbs. of milk and 352 lbs. of butter.

17256 Lady Bell 4th 84.

Calved July 8, 1901, bred and owned by John R. Valentine, Bryn Mawr, Pa.

Dam Lady Bell 14243; sire Oshawa of Highland 7225.

Home Dairy Test 1904-5; three years and 125 days old at beginning of test.

Record 8,516 lbs. of milk and 437 lbs. of butter.

18247 Kitty K 2d 85.

Calved June 12, 1902, bred and owned by John R. Valentine, Bryn Mawr, Pa.

Dam Kitty K 12933; sire Oshawa of Highland 7225.

Home Dairy Test 1905-6; three years and 159 days old at beginning of test.

Record 8,255 lbs. of milk and 411 lbs. of butter.

19350 Chatauqua Fairy 86.

Calved April 12, 1903, bred by C. E. Atwater & Son, East Avon, N. Y., owned by J. F. Butterfield Co., South Montrose, Pa.

Dam Chatauqua Girl 19349; sire Red Lad 8954.

Home Dairy Test 1906-7; three years and 195 days old at beginning of test.

Record 7,524 lbs. of milk and 356 lbs. of butter.

18681 Angeline Sebastian 87.

Calved October 23, 1902, bred and owned by J. F. Butterfield Co., South Montrose, Pa.

Dam Anna Webb 17454; sire Sebastian 6269.

Home Dairy Test 1906-7; three years and 205 days old at beginning of test.

Record 8,176 lbs. of milk and 397 lbs. of butter.

17360 Rotha of Ridgeside 88.

Calved May 9, 1902, bred by S. M. Wells, Newington, Conn., owned by Henry Dorrance, Plainfield, Conn.

Dam Rotha 2d 16175; sire Isaleigh Osborne of Castle Hill 6926.

Home Dairy Test 1906-7; three years and 206 days old at beginning of test.

Record 7,324 lbs. of milk and 386 lbs. of butter.

16351 Doris Y. 89.

Calved September 12, 1900, bred by James L. Young, Sterling, Conn., owned by Henry Dorrance, Plainfield, Conn.

Dam Musee Y 14839; sire Stonewall Douglas 6191.

Home Dairy Test 1904-5; three years and 216 days old at beginning of test.

Record 7,807 lbs. of milk and 365 lbs. of butter.

20324 Daisy Jewess 3d 90.

Calved October 25, 1902, bred and owned by L. A. Reymann, Wheeling, W. Va.

Dam Daisy Jewess 13333; sire Nox'emall 7312.

Home Dairy Test 1906-7; three years and 228 days old at beginning of test.

Record 9,665 lbs. of milk and 416 lbs. butter.

19833 Sweet Josie 91.

Calved December 23, 1902, bred by J. D. Honeyman, Portland, Oregon, owned by J. W. Clise, Redmond, Washington.

Dam Josie Douglas of Riverside 16238; sire Riverside-King 7315.

Home Dairy Test 1906-7; three years and 276 days old at beginning of test.

Record 10,103 lbs. of milk and 472 lbs. of butter.

22218 Broomhill Dairymaid 92.

Calved April, 1903, bred by Thomas Barbour, Scotland, owned by George H. McFadden, Bryn Mawr, Pa.

Dam Broomhill Milkmaid "19078"; sire Nethercraig High Tide "6329".

Home Dairy Test 1907-8; three years and 296 days old at beginning of test.

Record 8,326 lbs. of milk and 372 lbs. of butter.

17255 Nellie of Highland 93.

Calved October 22, 1901, bred and owned by John R. Valentine, Bryn Mawr, Pa.

Dam Nellie Dunken 14407; sire Oshawa of Highland 7225.

Home Dairy Test 1905-6; three years and 316 days old at beginning of test.

Record 8,374 lbs. of milk and 389 lbs. of butter.

22213 Babe's Duchess 94.

Calved November 28, 1902, bred and owned by L. A. Reymann, Wheeling, W. Va.

Dam Baby Jewess 14868; sire Nox'emall 7312.

Home Dairy Test 1906-7; three years and 350 days old at beginning of test.

Record 9,559 lbs. of milk and 452 lbs. of butter.

FOUR YEAR OLD FORM.

21622 Auchenbrain Princess 7th 95.

Calved April, 1902, bred by Robert Wallace, Scotland, owned by George H. McFadden, Bryn Mawr, Pa.

Dam Princess 5th of Auchenbrain "15010"; sire Rising Star of Auchenbrain "4583".

Home Dairy Test 1906-7; four years old at beginning of test.

Record 8,307 lbs. of milk and 405 lbs. of butter.

19217 Finlayston Maggie 3d 96.

Calved February, 1901, bred by Andrew Wilson, Scotland, owned by George H. McFadden, Bryn Mawr, Pa.

Dam Finlayston Maggie 2d "16953"; sire Burnock King of Finlayston "4573".

Home Dairy Test 1905-6; four years and 20 days old at beginning of test.

Record 10,759 lbs. of milk and 513 lbs. of butter.

21627 Broomhill Minnie 10th 97.

Calved April, 1902, bred by Thomas Barber, Scotland, owned by George H. McFadden, Bryn Mawr, Pa.

Dam Minnie 2d of Broomhill "11305"; sire General Buller of Broomhill "4352".

Home Dairy Test 1906-7; four years and 30 days old at beginning of test.

Record 9,409 lbs. of milk and 444 lbs. of butter

18679 Agnese Sebastian 98.

Calved May 30, 1902, bred and owned by J. F. Butterfield, South Montrose, Pa.

Dam Abbie Webb 17456; sire Sebastian 6269.

Home Dairy Test 1906-7; four years and 37 days old at beginning of test.

Record 9,364 lbs. of milk and 427 lbs. of butter.

17254 Ithan 2d 99.

Calved September 10, 1900, bred and owned by John R. Valentine, Bryn Mawr, Pa.

Dam Ithan 14538; sire Prince of Rome 6801.

Home Dairy Test 1904-5; four years and 47 days old at beginning of test.

Record 8,174 lbs. of milk and 430 lbs. of butter.

18678 Pauline Sebastian 100.

Calved May 18, 1902, bred and owned by J. F. Butterfield, South Montrose, Pa.

Dam Pet Webb 14682; sire Sebastian 6269.

Home Dairy Test 1906-7; four years and 50 days old at beginning of test.

Record 10,745 lbs. of milk and 422 lbs. of butter.

17473 Madonna Lass 2d 101.

Calved January 24, 1902, bred and owned by L. A. Reymann, Wheeling, W. Va.

Dam Madonna Lass 15986; sire Bill McDermott 7202.

Home Dairy Test 1906-7; four years and 76 days old at beginning of test.

Record 10,020 lbs. of milk and 449 lbs. of butter.

16779 Dollie Kilbowie 102.

Calved March 28, 1901, bred by C. M. Winslow & Son, Brandon, Vt., owned by Walter D. Turner, Moretown, Vt.

Dam Kate Kilbowie 15397; sire Twister 5651.

Home Dairy Test 1905-6; four years and 192 days old at beginning of test.

Record 9,039 lbs. of milk and 363 lbs. of butter.

15033 Lulu Avondale 24 (2d Entry).

Calved March 5, 1900, bred and owned by C. M. Winslow & Son, Brandon, Vt.

Dam Acelista 12094; sire Reynard 6038.

Home Dairy Test 1904-5; four years and 195 days old at beginning of test.

Record 8,326 lbs. of milk and 392 lbs. of butter.

17997 Miss Betty of Spring Hill 103.

Calved June 10, 1902, bred by Robert Hunter, Maxwell, Ont., owned by S. S. Karr, Almond, N. Y.

Dam Beauty of Spring Hill 17995; sire Glenora Mint 8283.

Home Dairy Test 1906-7; four years and 198 days old at beginning of test.

Record 8,334 lbs. of milk and 355 lbs. of butter.

17015 Beckey of Holehouse 104.

Calved April 17, 1900, bred by Robert Woodburn, Scotland, owned by George H. McFadden, Bryn Mawr, Pa.

Dam Horney of Holehouse 15580; sire Bright Smile of Nethercraig "4108".

Home Dairy Test 1905-6; four years and 314 days old at beginning of test.

Record 10,507 lbs. of milk and 463 lbs. of butter.

17024 Lizzie of Barclay 105.

Calved April 19, 1901, bred and owned by George H. McFadden, Bryn Mawr, Pa.

Dam Lizzie 6th of Auchenbrain 15583; sire Prince of Barclay 6711.

Home Dairy Test 1906-7; four years and 337 days old at beginning of test.

Record 8,868 lbs. of milk and 476 lbs. of butter.

MATURE COWS.

18645 Rose Pender 106.

Calved January 9, 1899, bred by H. S. Ayer, Columbus, Pa., owned by Howard Cook, Beloit, Ohio.

Dam Princess Beatrice 9667; sire Colonel Crawford 6997.

Home Dairy Test 1905-6.

Record 9,913 lbs. of milk and 416 lbs. of butter.

17461 Ada Rome 107.

Calved May 21, 1900, bred and owned by J. F. Butterfield, South Montrose, Pa.

Dam Ada Alexis 14675; sire Duke of Rome 6067.
Home Dairy Test 1906-7.
Record 9,835 lbs. of milk and 410 lbs. of butter.

15564 Ruby Russell 108.
Calved March 17, 1898, bred by Edward G. Palmer, Plainfield, Conn., owned by Henry Dorrance, Plainfield, Conn.
Dam Josie Russell 11227; sire Hillside Boy 6122.
Home Dairy Test 1904-5.
Record 8,643 lbs. of milk and 382 lbs. of butter.

16051 Molly Fryer 109.
Calved June 20, 1897, bred and owned by Henry Dorrance, Plainfield, Conn.
Dam Dolly Fryer 13012; sire Prince Lion 5624.
Home Dairy Test 1904-5.
Record 9,741 lbs. of milk and 453 lbs. of butter.

16286 Lady Sam. 110.
Calved July 6, 1899, bred by Edward G. Palmer, Plainfield, Conn., owned by Henry Dorrance, Plainfield, Conn.
Dam Nettie Lion 14856; sire Spotted Sam 6565.
Home Dairy Test 1905-6.
Record 9,530 lbs. of milk and 407 lbs. of butter.

13318 Alcyone of the Plain 111.
Calved June 24, 1894, bred by James E. Palmer, Stonington, Conn., owned by Connecticut Agricultural College, Storrs, Conn.
Dam Isabell D. 13316; sire Pekin 4955.
Connecticut Experiment Station 1905-6.
Record 8,646 lbs of milk and 377 lbs. of butter.

17861 Polly of Mauchlin 112.

Calved May, 1897, bred by Robert Wallace, Scotland, owned by Connecticut Agricultural College, Storrs, Conn.

Dam Beauty 7th of Auchenbrain "9991"; sire Sir Thomas of Auchenbrain "2760".

Connecticut Experiment Station 1903-4.

Record 9,321 lbs. of milk and 425 lbs. of butter.

16189 Lillian Drummond 4th 113.

Calved May 9, 1900, bred and owned by L. C. Spalding & Son, Poultney, Vt.

Dam Lillian Drummond 9403; sire Major Acme 6517.

Home Dairy Test 1906-7.

Record 9,239 lbs. of milk and 431 lbs. of butter.

14030 Hetty Ayer 114.

Calved March 11, 1897, bred by W. G. Tucker, Elm Valley, N. Y., owned by S. S. Karr & Sons, Almond, N. Y.

Dam Holly 12931; sire Major Ayer 5533.

Home Dairy Test 1907-8.

Record 9,858 lbs. of milk and 554 lbs. of butter.

15262 Bertha M 115.

Calved October 6, 1897, bred by Ira W. Jones, Alfred, N. Y., owned by S. S. Karr & Sons, Almond, N. Y.

Dam Nellie Clyde 12723; sire Major Ayer 5533.

Home Dairy Test 1906-7.

Record 8,754 lbs. of milk and 427 lbs. of butter.

18148 Etta Poultney 116

Calved August 3, 1901, bred by J. F. Converse, Woodville, N. Y., owned by J. W. Clise, Redmond, Washington.

Dam Myra of Poultney 16184; sire Nox'emall 7312.

Home Dairy Test 1906-7.

Record 11,475 lbs. of milk and 489 lbs. of butter.

20323 October Lass 117.

Calved October 12, 1902, bred by R. J. & W. J. Munce, Washington, Pa., owned by L. A. Reymann, Wheeling, W. Va.

Dam White Cordelia 12956; sire Happy Lad 8463.
Home Dairy Test 1907-8.
Record 10,078 lbs. of milk and 462 lbs. of butter.

17472 Daisy Jewess 2d 118.

Calved August 12, 1901, bred and owned by L. A. Reymann, Wheeling, W. Va.

Dam Daisy Jewess 13333; sire Twister 5651.
Home Dairy Test 1906-7.
Record 8,574 lbs. of milk and 393 lbs. of butter.

16152 Avis 119.

Calved September 5, 1900, bred by George H. Yeaton, Dover, N. H., owned by George F. Stone, Littleton, Mass.

Dam Yensie's Best 15138; sire Solitaire 6548.
Home Dairy Test 1906-7.
Record 9,424 lbs. of milk and 378 lbs. of butter.

13715 Crimsonia 2d 120.

Calved August 24, 1898, bred by Anson C. Piper, South Acton, Mass., owned by George F. Stone, Littleton, Mass.

Dam Crimsonia 12341; sire Vinewood Drummond 5707.
Home Dairy Test 1906-7.
Record 9,645 lbs. of milk and 417 lbs. of butter.

16466 Mary A. M. 2d 121.

Calved April 15, 1898, bred and owned by A. B. McConnell, Wellington, Ohio.

Dam Mary A. M. 12503; sire Jo Smith 7398.
Home Dairy Test 1906-7.
Record 9,782 lbs. of milk and 400 lbs. of butter.

16538 Clarrissa Lorain 122.
Calved March 17, 1897, bred and owned by A. B. McConnell, Wellington, Ohio.
Dam Clara Lorain 2d 16465; sire Jo Smith 7398.
Home Dairy Test 1906-7.
Record 9,051 lbs. of milk and 384 lbs. of butter.

12773 Iola Lorne 17 (2d entry).
Calved October 30, 1894, bred and owned by C. M. Winslow & Son, Brandon, Vt.
Dam Atalanta 10777; sire Nonpareil 4535.
Home Dairy Test 1904-5.
Record 9,675 lbs. of milk and 394 lbs. of butter.

12094 Acelista 8 (2d entry).
Calved September 20, 1894, bred and owned by C. M. Winslow & Son, Brandon, Vt.
Dam Acme 5th 10342; sire Nonpareil 4535.
Home Dairy Test 1904-5.
Record 11,856 lbs. of milk and 489 lbs. of butter.

15874 Miss Mabel D 123
Calved May 24, 1894, bred by Oliver Smith, Chateaugay, N. Y., owned by C. M. Winslow & Son, Brandon, Vt.
Dam Miss Mabel 2d 11322; sire Beppo 4678.
Home Dairy Test 1905-6.
Record 9,693 lbs. of milk and 408 lbs. of butter.

16296 Polly Puss 124.
Calved February 12, 1900, bred by W. G. Tucker, Elm Valley, N. Y., owned by John R. Valentine, Bryn Mawr, Pa.

Dam Polly J 15238; sire Major Ayer 5533.
Home Dairy Test 1905-6.
Record 12632 lbs. of milk and 584 lbs. of butter.

16289 Fern Ayer 125

Calved February 10, 1899, bred by W. G. Tucker, Elm Valley, N. Y., owned by John R. Valentine, Bryn Mawr, Pa.

Dam Favorite Princess 13990; sire Major Ayer 5533.
Home Dairy Test 1905-6.
Record 9,847 lbs. of milk and 444 lbs. of butter.

12479 Rena Webb 126

Calved September 25, 1892, bred by W. G. Tucker, Elm Valley, N. Y., owned by John R. Valentine, Bryn Mawr, Pa.

Dam Rena Clyde 10051; sire Sir Webb 4658.
Home Dairy Test 1905-6.
Record 9,366 lbs. of milk and 425 lbs. of butter.

16020 Oshawa Lady 127.

Calved March 31, 1898, bred by estate of Thomas Guy, Oshawa, Ont., owned by John R. Valentine, Bryn Mawr, Pa.

Dam Oshawa Lass 7th 14239; sire Eva's Heir 7197.
Home Dairy Test 1905-6.
Record 9,695 lbs. of milk and 404 lbs. of butter.

16536 Lady Bell 2d 128.

Calved August 19, 1899, bred and owned by John R. Valentine, Bryn Mawr, Pa.

Dam Lady Bell 14243; sire Tam Oshanta 6705.
Home Dairy Test 1906-7.
Record 8,628 lbs. of milk and 416 lbs. of butter.

16534 Oshawa Lass of Highland 129.

Calved August 1, 1899, bred and owned by John R. Valentine, Bryn Mawr, Pa.

Dam Oshawa Lass 6th 14238; sire Tam Oshanta 6705.

Home Dairy Test 1905-6.

Record 8,561.3 lbs. of milk and 378 lbs. of butter.

12933 Kitty K 130.

Calved May 30, 1894, bred by W. G. Tucker, Elm Valley, N. Y., owned by John R. Valentine, Bryn Mawr, Pa.

Dam Kalley 12660; sire Jacob 5602.

Home Dairy Test 1905-6.

Record 11,115 lbs. of milk and 512 lbs. of butter.

15913 Keepsake 131.

Calved September 30, 1898, bred by W. G. Tucker, Elm Valley, N. Y., owned by John R. Valentine, Bryn Mawr, Pa.

Dam Kalley 12660; sire Major Ayer 5533.

Home Dairy Test 1905-6.

Record 10,868 lbs. of milk and 513 lbs. of butter.

14539 Rena Ross 132.

Calved February 28, 1898, bred by W. G. Tucker, Elm Valley, N. Y., owned by John R. Valentine, Bryn Mawr, Pa.

Dam Rena Webb 12479; sire Major Ayer 5533.

Home Dairy Test 1904-5.

Record 10,065 lbs. of milk and 512 lbs. of butter.

14538 Ithan 133.

Calved January 28, 1898, bred by W. G. Tucker, Elm Valley, N. Y., owned by John R. Valentine, Bryn Mawr, Pa.

Dam Iola Webb 12477; sire Major Ayer 5533.
Home Dairy Test 1905-6.
Record 9,975 lbs. of milk and 463 lbs. of butter.

15578 Flora 4th of Bonshaw 134.

Calved April, 1896, bred by Robert M. Reid, Bonshaw, Scotland, owned by George H. McFadden, Bryn Mawr, Pa.

Dam Flora 1st of Bonshaw "12674"; sire Royal Kyle of Bonshaw "3119".

Home Dairy Test 1905-6.

Record 9,874 lbs. of milk and 435 lbs. of butter.

17018 Friskey of Bonshaw 135.

Calved January 16, 1901, bred and owned by George H. McFadden, Bryn Mawr, Pa.

Dam Cherry of Bonshaw 15582; sire Prince of Barclay 6711.

Home Dairy Test 1906-7.

Record 8,767 lbs. of milk and 436 lbs. of butter.

17013 Maggie of Radnor 136.

Calved February 26, 1900, bred by Robert M. Reid, Bonshaw, Scotland, owned by George H. McFadden, Bryn Mawr, Pa.

Dam Flora 4th of Bonshaw 15578; sire Shamrock of Bonshaw "4200".

Home Dairy Test 1905-6.

Record 9,468 lbs. of milk and 474 lbs. of butter.

15577 Denty 9th of Auchenbrain 137.

Calved April, 1896, bred by Robert Wallace, Mauchline, Scotland, owned by George H. McFadden, Bryn Mawr, Pa.

Dam Denty 6th of Auchenbrain "5569"; sire Sir Thomas of Auchenbrain "2760".

Home Dairy Test 1905-6.
Record 11,757 lbs. of milk and 528 lbs. of butter.

17011 Daisy of Rosemont 138.

Calved February 13, 1900, bred by Robert Woodburn, Holehouse, Scotland, owned by George H. McFadden, Bryn Mawr, Pa.

Dam Lady Stair of Holehouse 15574, imp.; sire Traveller's Heir "2903".

Home Dairy Test 1906-7.
Record 9,164 lbs. of milk and 397 lbs. of butter.

15096 Queen of Barclay 139.

Calved May 5, 1898, bred by James Robb, Hindsward, Scotland, owned by George H. McFadden, Bryn Mawr, Pa.

Dam Mosshawk of Hindsward 15095, imp.; sire Lord Nelson of Ardgowan "3607".

Home Dairy Test 1905-6.
Record 9,172 lbs. of milk and 399 lbs. of butter.

15579 Lily 4th of Fairfield Mains 140.

Calved February, 1897, bred by Thomas Howie, Monkton, Scotland, owned by George H. McFadden, Bryn Mawr, Pa.

Dam Lily 1st of Fairfield Mains "12654"; sire Baron's Heir of Fairfield Mains "3837".

Home Dairy Test 1905-6.
Record 9,054 lbs. of milk and 400 lbs. of butter.

19216 Brown Eyes of Knockdon 141.

Calved April 27, 1899, bred by Alexander Cross, Knockdon, Scotland, owned by George H. McFadden, Bryn Mawr, Pa.

Dam Bright Eyes 4th of Knockdon "10517"; sire Yellow Squire of Castlehill "2912".

Home Dairy Test 1906-7.

Record 8,724 lbs. of milk and 413 lbs. of butter.

15105 Lady Browning 142.

Calved November 3, 1898, bred and owned by George H. McFadden, Bryn Mawr, Pa.

Dam Kirsty 7th of Auchenbrain 15093, imp.; sire Royalty of Monkland 6704, imp.

Home Dairy Test 1906-7.

Record 8,531 lbs. of milk and 375 lbs. of butter.

17018 Friskey of Bonshaw 135 (2d entry).

Calved January 16, 1901, bred and owned by George H. McFadden, Bryn Mawr, Pa.

Dam Cherry of Bonshaw 15582; sire Prince of Barclay 6711.

Home Dairy Test 1907-8.

Record 9,645 lbs of milk and 463 lbs. of butter.

15096 Queen of Barclay 139 (2d entry).

Calved May 5, 1898, bred by James Robb, Scotland, owned by George H. McFadden, Bryn Mawr, Pa.

Dam Mosshawk of Hindsward 15095, imp.; sire Lord Nelson of Ardgowan "3607."

Home Dairy Test 1907-8.

Record 11,258 lbs. of milk and 484 lbs. of butter.

21628 Clockston Bella 2d 143.

Calved May, 1901, bred by Robert Meikle, Scotland, owned by George H. McFadden, Bryn Mawr, Pa.

Dam Bella of Clockston "10248"; sire Ailsa of Kirkchrist "3538."

Home Dairy Test 1907-8.

Record 8,509 lbs. of milk and 412 lbs. of butter.

13984 Miss Olga 144.

Calved March 24, 1896, bred and owned by George H. Yeaton, Dover, N. H.

Dam Olah 11471; sire Lord Mar 5134.

Home Dairy Test 1904-5.

Record 10,200 lbs. of milk and 451 lbs. of butter.

12351 Biona 145.

Calved October 15, 1892, bred and owned by George H. Yeaton, Dover, N. H.

Dam Annie Bert 9670; sire Calmar 4692.

Home Dairy Test 1904-5.

Record 10,012 lbs. of milk and 394 lbs. of butter.

CONNECTICUT AND INDIANA

HOMEHILL FARM

AYRSHIRES FOR BUSINESS

Improve your herd by buying bulls that are descended from Advanced Registry stock.

We have seven cows admitted to Advanced Registry from which we offer stock for sale.

Our stock bull is out of Polly of Mauchlin, imp., who qualified for Advanced Registry with a year's record of 9321 lbs. of milk and 425 lbs. of butter and dropped a calf 14 months from the beginning of the test.

HENRY DORRANCE, Prop.

Plainfield, - - - - - - - **Conn.**

INDIANA AYRSHIRES

Bull calves and young bulls for sale, at reasonable prices. No heifers. Herd rich in the blood of Glencairn 3rd, No. 6247, imp., White Floss, No. 1334, Duke of Barcheskie, No. 8305, Chief I Am, No. 7954 and Clover King, No. 8232.

C. C. RICHARDS

Malott Park - - - - - **Ind.**

HILL VIEW FARM
AYRSHIRES

Headed by such bulls as Sachs No. 8160, a fine individual and closely related to Lady Fox and Rena Myrtle and a long line of heavy producers; also the promising young bull Moonshine of Barclay 10261. Our three herds number about 75 head.

YOUNG BULL CALVES AND A FEW HEIFERS FOR SALE AT ALL TIMES

We give a square deal to all purchasers. Good shipping facilities to all parts. 35 miles south-west of Cleveland. Over 20 years building this herd. Visitors met at electric stop or at railway.

ADDRESS—

A. B. McCONNELL & SONS
Wellington, - - - - - Ohio

MAPLE GROVE FARM
AYRSHIRES

Our herd was established in 1904, carefully selected from the herd of R. R. Ness, Howick, Que., Canada, numbering now (40) forty head. The cows are of good size, with large teats, and good producers. The bulls used have been selected with the greatest care, Imp. Duke Clarence of Barcheskie heading the herd for two years, and now by Imp. Barcheskie's Copestone, who gives promise of being a great breeder and who won the Grand Championship at Brockton Fair, 1907. Animals of all ages and both sexes for sale.

The farm is located one mile from the M. C. R. R. and G. T. R. stations, electrics running by the farm. Long distance phone. Correspondence and inspection invited.

J. A. & ROWLAND NESS
Auburn - - - - - - - Me.

BELL FARM AYRSHIRES

Herd headed by Hollis Martinot No. 9045. Two of his half sisters in the herd. Yucca Douglas No. 19504 as a two-year-old gave 7,412 lbs. milk and Esthon Douglas No. 19153 as a three-year-old gave 8,663 lbs. milk in a year.

STOCK FOR SALE AT REASONABLE PRICES

CHAS. J. BELL, HOLLIS, N. H.

L. W. WHIPPLE & SONS
MALONE, N.Y.

Herd of Ayrshires are all direct from late Scotch importations.

We have spared neither pains nor expense to get the best. We shall have a limited number of calves of both sexes for sale at very reasonable prices considering the breeding.

LET US SELECT FOR YOU AND WE ARE SURE WE CAN PLEASE YOU WITH QUALITY AND SURPRISE YOU IN PRICE

SUNNYSIDE STOCK FARM
HOME OF THE AYRSHIRES

Cows of the celebrated Ayer family, of strong, rugged constitution, rich, deep milkers, with teats that a man can milk.

THE HERD BULL
JEAN CANUCK

His dam, Jean Armour, one of Canada's grand cows, with extra long teats, wide set on a perfect Ayrshire udder. This cow has given 60 lbs. milk per day for 60 days, testing four per cent butter fat.

YOUNG STOCK FOR SALE
C. W. LEWIS & SONS, Props.
Alfred Station, N. Y.

NEW YORK

Riverside Ayrshires

HOWIES FIZZAWAY

100 Head, marshalled by the imported bull Howie's Fizzaway, champion of two continents. This herd holds the record of the largest exposition of PRIZE RIBBONS of any herd in America.

STOCK OF QUALITY FOR SALE AT TEMPTING PRICES

Address—
J. F. CONVERSE & CO.
WOODVILLE, N. Y.

NEW YORK

CLOVER HOME FARM

GOUVERNEUR, : : : : NEW YORK

REGISTERED AYRSHIRES

The home of over sixty head of registered Ayrshires that have been bred and fed for profitable dairy results. : : : : :

We breed for size as well as all dairy qualities, and haven't a short-teated cow in the bunch. : : : : : : :

Two bulls of incomparable breeding now head the herd:—

DREW'S FAVORITE No. 9276, a grandson of the famous butter cow—MISS OLLIE—and pronounced by his breeder, the late L. S. DREW, "*The best bull I ever bred.*"

JACK MACDONALD, No. 10259, a grandson of the imported DENTY 9th of AUCHENBRAIN, whose official record is 11,757 lbs. milk, 528 lbs. butter, and recently sold at National Dairy show at advertised price of $1,155.00. : : : : :

We are offering this year all of our best calves without reservation. : : : :

HERD TUBERCULIN TESTED

GEORGE E. PIKE

Gouverneur, New York

Long Distance Bell Telephone :-: :-: :-: :-: :-: :-:
:-: :-: :-: :-: :-: Reference, Bank of Gouverneur

NEW YORK

M. J. KARR   S. S. KARR   I. D. KARR

SAND HILL STOCK FARM

S. S. KARR & SONS

Allegany Co.   **Almond, N. Y.**

Our herd consists of 70 choice cows and heifers. The cows are of good size, with good udders and teats, and are proving themselves very good producers by their official records.

Among them are Polly J. 15238, which is the dam of Polly Puss 16296, the champion milk and butter cow.

Prudence Ayr 17160, a full sister of Polly Puss.

Four daughters of Polly J. and four cows sired by Major Ayer 5533, who sired Polly Puss and has several descendants in the Advanced Registry.

We have also four cows bred by Robt. Hunter & Sons.

The following cows have qualified for Advanced Registry the past year:

Name	Number	Age	Lbs. Milk	Lbs. Butter
Isabella of Sand Hill	20366	2	7,887	373
Bessie of Sand Hill	20365	2	7,307	376
Midget of Sand Hill	19487	3	9,824	422
Miss Betty of Spring Hill	17997	4	8,334	355
Hetty Ayr	14030	10	9,694	542
Grace of Sand Hill	22472	2	7,990	358

The last two, Hetty Ayr and Grace of Sand Hill, have been in test only 11 months.

We are now testing 11 head which have made records good enough to assure their entering, with one exception.

Our herd bulls are Earl's Choice of Spring Hill 8289, sire Stately's Heir of Muir 8288, imp. Dam. Wee Maggie 17996; Bannerman of Spring Hill 9727, sire Lessnessock King of Beauty 9726 imp., dam Eoline of Glenhurst 20949. Both bulls were bred by Robert Hunter & Sons, Maxville.

Earl's Choice is a fine bull and has proven himself an extra good breeder. He is the sire of Isabella and Grace.

Bannerman is a very nice, showy young bull.

We have a few young cows and heifers for sale; also some bull calves, among them is one from Midget and one from Prudence Ayr, both sired by Earl's Choice.

We are located on the Erie R. R. about one mile from Almond station, and five miles from city of Hornell.

HERD TUBERCULIN TESTED.   VISITORS WELCOME

NEW YORK

MAPLE ROW STOCK FARM

AYRSHIRES

We have 75 head of Ayrshires of all ages and keep none that will not fill the bill in the dairy, as they must be milkers or leave the farm.

STOCK OF ALL AGES FOR SALE AT REASONABLE PRICES. CORRESPONDENCE SOLICITED

F. H. COOKINGHAM, Cherry Creek, N. Y.

E. TEN EYCK LANSING

LITTLE FALLS — — — — — N. Y.

Member Ayrshire Breeders' Association, Member D.H.S.B.A. of America.

Descendants of Rose Cleon, Acelista, Miss Ollie, Lady Fox and Cock-a-Bendie

Dairy, not show type, has been the desideratum

BULL CALVES FOR SALE AT FARMER'S PRICES

G. L. RODGER

BREEDER OF AYRSHIRE CATTLE

ROCK RIDGE FARM

GOUVERNEUR, N. Y.

PENNSYLVANIA AND NEW YORK

HIGHLAND FARM

JOHN R. VALENTINE, Proprietor

Home of Polly Puss, Champion Ayrshire cow for milk and butter of the world. Keepsake Home Dairy Test winner of 1906. Herd headed by two great sires. Colonel Ayer 7168 (advanced reg.), half brother to Polly Puss, Keepsake and Rena Ross. Sire of six daughters in the list and many more qualifying. Imported Finlaystone 8882, dam Finlaystone Maggie 3rd 19217, Champion four-year-old cow of the world for milk and butter and sold at auction for $600.00.

The following are the Official Records of the Herd since 1905:—

Name	Number	Lbs. of Milk	Lbs. of Butter
Polly Puss	16296	12,632	584
Keepsake	15913	10,868	513
Rena Ross	14539	10,065	512
Kitty K.	12933	11,115	512
Ithan	14538	9,975	463
Fern Ayer	16289	9,847	444
Rena Webb	12479	9,336	425
Lady Bell 2nd	16535	8,628	416
Oshawa Lady	16020	9,659	404
Oshawa Lass of Highland	16534	8,561	378
Ithan 2nd, 4 years old	17254	8,174	430
THREE YEARS OLD			
Lady Bell 4th	17256	8,516	437
Kitty K. 2nd	18247	8,255	411
Nellie of Highland	17255	8,374	389
Kaziah 2nd	20181	—	—
TWO YEARS OLD			
Kitty K. 3rd	21246	—	—
Bell Ayer	20180	7,111	361
Oshawa Lady 2nd	18249	7,074	356
Rena Ayer	21247	—	—
Felicia of Woodview	17431	7,049	326
Neidpath Lassie 2nd	18248	6,746	301

Farm located nine miles west of Philadelphia, on the main line of the Penn. R. R.

PHILIP C. PALMER, Manager

Highland Farm — — — — Bryn Mawr, Pa.

AYRSHIRES

Herd Established in 1871

All ages, both sexes, bred for practical dairy purposes, size, constitution, disposition, style, length of teat and deep and persistent milkers.

SINGLE ANIMALS OR CAR LOTS

F. D. & E. STOWELL, Successors to L. D. Stowell

Black Creek, Allegany Co., N. Y.

VERMONT

High Class Ayrshire Cattle

HERD BELONGING TO THE LATE L. S. DREW
FOUNDED IN 1865

Choice Cows, Heifers and Calves for Sale. Reasonable Prices.

F. A. DREW, So. Burlington, Vt.

HILLCROFT FARM

BROWNSVILLE — — VERMONT

Ayrshire Cattle
(REGISTERED)

FOR SALE AT ALL TIMES

Herd headed by Frisky 9221, winner of 27 first prizes and Champion at Vermont State Fair; also first prize Herd and Champion cow at Vermont State Fair.

HERD FREE FROM TUBERCULOSIS

MATTHEW HANNAH

VERMONT

1873 ———————————————— *1908*

C. M. WINSLOW & SON
BRANDON - - - VERMONT

**FARM SITUATED NEAR
THE RAILROAD STATION**

HERD FREE FROM TUBERCULOSIS

This herd was established in 1873 by purchase of a few heifers from cows that had strong constitutions, were typical animals of the breed, had shapely udders and long teats.

These families have been bred on the farm since then, with care in selecting bulls, to perpetuate the desirable qualities found in the Ayrshire cow.

As the herd stands today, they are dark red and white, white and dark red, small upright horns, shapely bodies, of good size, typical udders with long teats and have a quiet disposition.

They have been bred from the start for a profitable dairy herd that should be good feeders and good milkers.

YOUNG STOCK FOR SALE

PENNSYLVANIA AND VERMONT

"AYRMONT FARM"
AYRSHIRE HERD

ESTABLISHED 1869 ———————————— TUBERCULOSIS FREE

Duke of Netherhall 9682 at head of herd. His dam Beckey of Holehouse 17015 (imp.) made 10,507 lbs. milk and 463 lbs. butter in one year (official), second prize home dairy test on five cows in 1907. Five in the Advanced Registry as follows:—

Ada Rome 17461,   6 yrs., 9,835 lbs. milk, 410 lbs. butter in year
Pauline Sebastian 18678, 4 "   10,745   "   422   "   "
Agnese   " 18679, 4 "   9,364   "   427   "   "
Angeline   " 18681, 3 "   8,176   "   396   "   "
Chautauqua Fairy 19350, 3 "   7,524   "   356   "   "

BULL CALVES, HEIFERS AND A FEW COWS FOR SALE
PRICES AS TO QUALITY

Address:—

DR. J. F. BUTTERFIELD
SOUTH MONTROSE, PENN.

BROOKLAWN HERD

ESTABLISHED 1869

L. C. SPALDING & SON

POULTNEY ·· ·· ·· VERMONT

Young Bulls Fit for Service
from Producing Dams for Sale.

YOUNG CALVES A SPECIALTY

INSPECTION INVITED

PENNSYLVANIA

PENSHURST AYRSHIRES
BRED FOR
MILK, BUTTER AND SHOW
BULLS IN SERVICE

LESSNESSOCK KING OF BEAUTY 9726, imp., probably the greatest show and breeding bull ever imported. He won in 1905 1st and Championship Ottawa and Toronto, headed 1st prize herd, sired 1st prize young herd, 1st prize senior bull calf, 1st, 2nd and 3rd prize senior heifer calves and 1st prize junior heifer calf, an unequalled record. His dam, Queen of Beauty of Carsegowan, milked 60 lbs. in a day, won numerous 1st prizes and is perhaps the greatest breeding cow of her day.

LESSNESSOCK DOUGLAS MONARCH 10020, imp., was selected to breed to King's daughters, after a careful search of all Scotland, as he came the nearest to filling our ideal as a sire of milk, butter and prize winners. His sire is that great show and breeding bull, Howie's Merry Monarch, dam Kate 8th of Netherhall, milked 63 lbs. in a day and won wherever shown.

In the herd are such cows as Garclaugh Bloomer 2nd, never beaten in show ring; Kirkland Sparrow, official weekly test 382.2 lbs. milk, 18 lbs. butter; Primrose, official yearly test 10325 lbs. milk, 450 lbs. butter, and many others equally good.

If in need of Big Milkers, large Butter Makers or animals to win in the Show Ring, come or write to

PENSHURST FARM, NARBERTH, Pa.

P.S.---Narberth is seven miles west of Philadelphia on main line Pennsylvania R. R.

"Hill Top Farm"
AYRSHIRES

Herd headed by the Advance Registry sire Nox'emall 7312. His heifers are being bred to the sensational prize-winner Howie's Dairy King (imp.) "5707" 9855.

The females composing this herd are about 80 in number, all typical. Among them are many prize winners and Advance Registry animals. The sensational two-year-old Champion Baby Douglas was bred and is still at Hill Top Farm.

L. A. REYMANN

Wheeling - - - W. Va.

NATIONAL DAIRY SHOW, CHICAGO, 1907.

MYRTLE DELL OF CHATEAUGAY 15884.

NATIONAL DAIRY SHOW, CHICAGO, 1907.

AUCHENBRAIN WHITE BEAUTY 2D 21687.

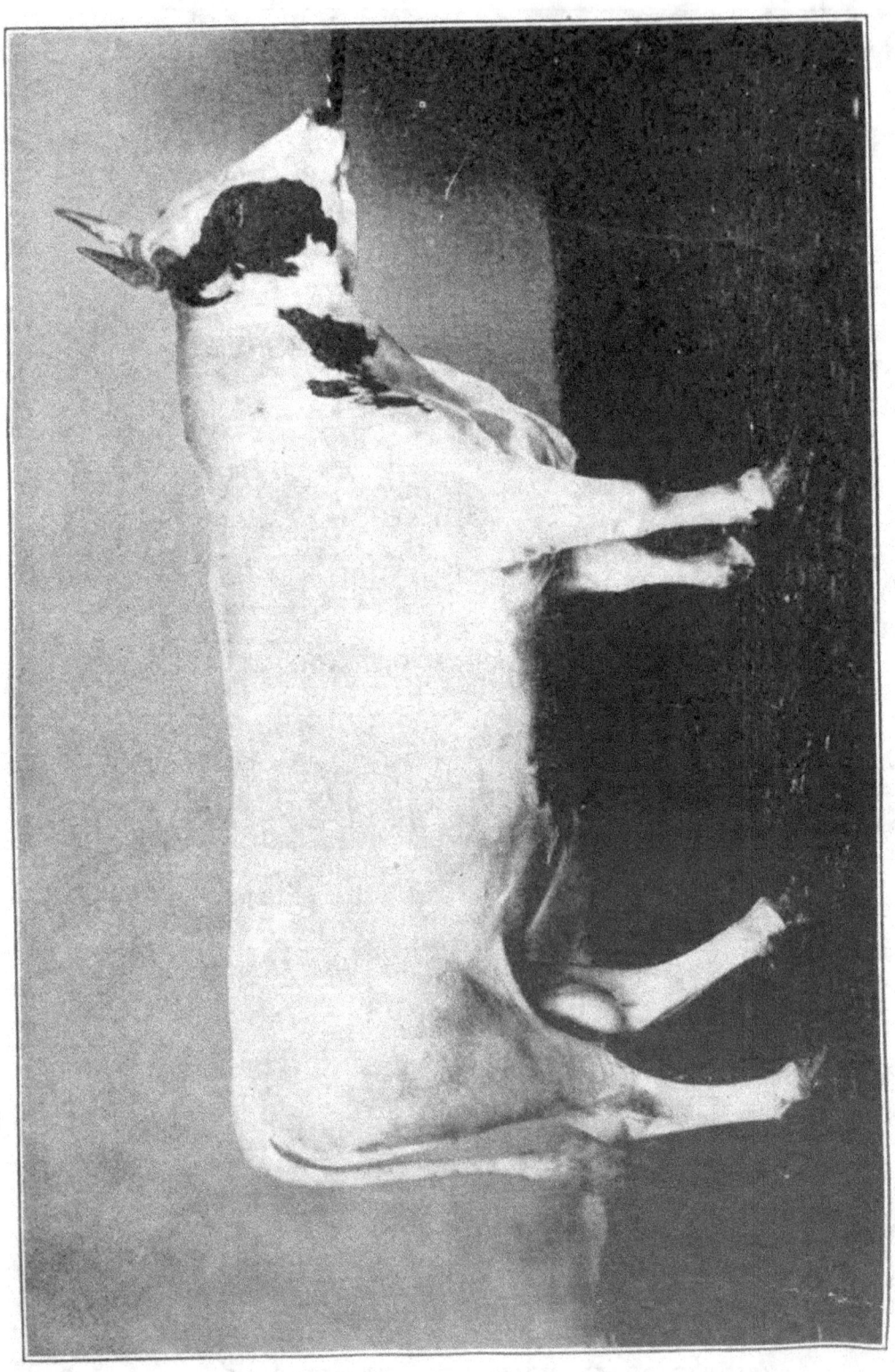

HOWIE'S MAJESTIC 10000.
Grand Champion at Illinois State Fair, 1907. Second at National Dairy Show.

22218 BROOMHILL DAIRYMAID, A. R. 92.
Owned by George H. McFadden, Bryn Mawr, Pa. Record in the Three-Year Old Form: 8,326 Lbs. of Milk and 372 Lbs. of Butter.

8228 MOONSTONE OF DRUMSUIE, A. R. 7.
Sire of 4 in the List.

FIRST PRIZE HERD AT NEW HAMPSHIRE STATE FAIR.

7312 NOX'EMALL, A. R. 6.
Owned by L. A. Reymann, Wheeling, W. Va.
Four in the List.

20511 ROSE EATON, A. R. 73.
Owned by C. M. Winslow & Son, Brandon, Vt. Record in the Two-Year
Old Form: 7,783 Lbs. of Milk and 324 Lbs. of Butter in One Year.

18824 ORINDA, A. R. 78.
Owned by J. W. Clise, Redmond, Wash. Record in Three-Year Old Form: 7,375 Lbs. of Milk and 327 Lbs. of Butter in One Year.

19754 BONNIE 2D OF RADNOR, A. R. 40.
Owned by J. W. Clise, Redmond, Wash. Record in Two-Year Old Form: 8,184 Lbs. of Milk and 403 Lbs. of Butter.

18821 LADY ROTHA, A. R. 75.
Owned by J. W. Clise, Redmond, Wash. Record in Three-Year Old Form: 8101 Lbs. of Milk and 368 Lbs. of Butter in One Year.

19748 QUEEN 2D OF BARCLAY, A. R. 57.
Owned by J. W. Clise, Redmond, Wash. Record in Two-Year Old Form: 9,486 Lbs. of Milk and 425 Lbs. of Butter in One Year.

NATIONAL DAIRY SHOW, CHICAGO, 1907.

PITTSFORD MODEL AT 8 MONTHS.

NATIONAL DAIRY SHOW, CHICAGO, 1907.

LILLIAN D. DRUMMOND 21881.

DOUGLAS GIRL 21882.

NATIONAL DAIRY SHOW, CHICAGO, 1907.

FIRST PRIZE HERD AT VERMONT STATE FAIR, 1907.

BARCLAY FARM—AYRSHIRE COWS.

6180 DUKE OF AYER, A. R. 4.
Owned by W. V. Probasco, Cream Ridge, N. J.
Four in the List.

15913 KEEPSAKE, A. R. 131.
Owned by John R. Valentine, Bryn Mawr, Pa. Record as a Mature Cow: 10,868 Lbs. of Milk and 513 Lbs. of Butter in One Year.

NATIONAL DAIRY SHOW, CHICAGO, 1907.

20951 KIRKLAND SPARROW, A. R. 37.
Owned by Percival Roberts, Jr., Narberth, Pa. Seven Day Record: 382.2 Lbs. of Milk and 17.7782 Lbs. of Butter.

NATIONAL DAIRY SHOW, CHICAGO, 1907.

REBA #15907

UARDA 15135.

www.ingramcontent.com/pod-product-compliance
Lightning Source LLC
Chambersburg PA
CBHW082327220526
45470CB00008B/2426